CREATIVE ROLE PLAY
IN THE EARLY YEARS

How to plan stimulating and exciting role play, inside and out!

Published 2013 by Featherstone Education
Bloomsbury Publishing Plc
50 Bedford Square, London, WC1B 3DP
www.bloomsbury.com

ISBN 978-1-4081-5547-9

A CIP catalogue for this book is available from the British Library.

Printed and bound in India by Replika Press Pvt. Ltd

10 9 8 7 6 5 4 3 2 1

This book is produced using paper that is made from wood grown in
managed, sustainable forests. It is natural, renewable and recyclable.
The logging and manufacturing process conform to the environmental
regulations of the country of origin.

To see our full range of titles visit www.bloomsbury.com

Thank you to all the children and practitioners whose images appear in
this book with special mention to: Fee Bryce-Clegg, TTS, Cool Canvas,
Infinite Playgrounds, The Friars Primary School, Moorside Primary School,
Saint Andrew's Primary School, Middlefield Primary School, Little 1's
Nursery, Chester Blue Coat Primary, Noah's Ark Pre School, Claremont
Primary School, Ladybrook Primary School, Stanley Primary School, Acorn
Childcare Ltd, Milton Keynes.

Contents

Preface

> Turn to the person next to you and ...

In my role as an early years consultant I deliver lots of training at various conferences. Not only does this make me an expert in manoeuvring my way through a buffet, but it also allows me to sneak in and watch the other speakers delivering their training. What I am not very good at is sitting still and listening for long periods of time, so I know if someone has delivered their message well if the time flies by and I haven't worn the velour off my seat by shuffling on it!

Having said that, I would rather be bored than asked to engage in any form of paired or group role play! My heart literally sinks when I hear the immortal words: 'Now, I want you to turn to the person next to you and …'. This has happened to me so many times that I now find myself consciously checking out the person next to me and mentally preparing myself for the myriad of paired scenarios that might be ahead of us.

Once I have ascertained, to the best of my ability, that I haven't chosen to sit next to a serial killer (although I appreciate it can be difficult to tell) I then begin my own mantra of personal paranoia. When did I last eat garlic? Have I got something sticking out of my nose that they can see but I can't? As soon as anyone I am talking to scratches or rubs their nose, I fear the worst. My head is telling me that they are giving me a subliminal signal that I have. This causes me then to rub my nose, which in turn prompts them to think that I am trying to tell them that they have something up their nose. So it goes on until you find that you have spent the last 30 minutes engaged in synchronised nose rubbing, for no reason. The whole thing is an absolute minefield!

I think I was scarred by the 'turn to the person next to you' role play syndrome early on in my teaching career when I went to see a very high profile education consultant speak. I was one of many who crammed into a conference hall and sat in seats that had been placed far too close together for my liking and personal comfort (I was involuntarily touching upper thighs with the person on either side of me, not something I would normally do with someone I have never met before). All was going well (apart from the thigh thing) until we got to the role play 'peer massage' section of the day. At this point in my career I was a 'turn to the person next to you' virgin so had no idea what was about to happen which made the resulting activity even more traumatic.

The consultant in question said 'I would never ask a child to do something that I wasn't prepared to do myself, and neither should you'. While I was considering the enormity of that statement and the impact that it could have on my physical well-being teaching a reception class, she then uttered those words: 'So, turn to the person on your left and place your hands on their shoulders'. At first I thought she might be joking, but she wasn't! I then thought that perhaps everyone else in the room would be feeling the same huge sense of horror and despair that I was. But they weren't! Instead of an audible groan and a mass refusal to take part, there was a significant amount of whooping and over exaggerated 'mum laughing' (the sort mums do when meeting new people for the first time that can often be mistaken for a chicken about to lay)!

The first thing I noticed about the person on my left was the 'kittens playing with a ball of wool' design on her fleece (well, it was an early years conference) quickly followed by the copious amounts of fur from what I can only assume were real kittens that gave sections of the said fleece more of a mohair appearance. But, like a dutiful delegate I laid my hands on her shoulders. What with the hands and the thighs, I had had more bodily contact with this woman in an hour than I had with most girlfriends on the third date.

Of course if I was laying my hands on the 'kitten lady', someone must be laying theirs on me. At first this didn't seem too bad, but as the peer massage began it turned out I had the sister of Edward Scissorhands, who seemed intent

on not only finding but breaking every bone in my shoulders! As for the 'kitten lady', she decided it would be hilarious to re-enact that famous Meg Ryan scene in a very vocal fashion as I rubbed her shoulders wanting the ground to open up and swallow me more than ever before (or since).

So, if someone on a conference mentions the words 'role play' or asks you to turn to the person next to you, my advice is to run and run fast! Oh, and never sit next to anyone in a kitten fleece. Ever! In my experience, a lot of children can feel a bit the same when role play is 'thrust' upon them. Although they can benefit from some scaffolding and structure for their play, children tend to respond better if their role play is organic and comes from them. Some subtle theming around interests or events can help to enhance their play, but the more open ended and 'ambiguous' the role play space and topic the more room you give them to explore all the skills associated with effective role playing.

When children are 'grouped' by an adult for a role playing experience, then you risk stifling their success by putting them with someone who they are not comfortable playing alongside or someone they just don't get along with. Playing with your friends can foster a high level of engagement and joy. Playing with someone

you are not as comfortable with, is not going to support you in suspending your disbelief and enhancing your learning.

Good role play encourages children to revisit, explore and expand their learning and experiences. The more comfortable they are in the role play spaces that you create, the more effective their learning will be.

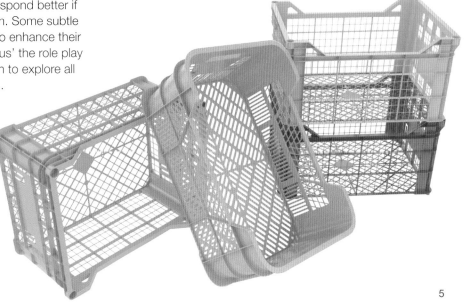

Why do we role play?

The truth is, it is not just us humans who engage in role play as an important part of our learning and development. The animal kingdom is full of species that spend a great deal of their time playing to learn and learning to play. Play is crucial to our social development: it helps us to become familiar with our own preferences and feelings, as well as helping us learn to recognise other people's emotional states. Without opportunities for role play we would not get the chance to observe, practise and rehearse the subtleties of social signaling which make us effective and appropriate communicators.

Research has shown that active play selectively stimulates the brain derived neurotropic factor which stimulates nerve growth in the amygdala (where emotions are processed) and the dorsolateral prefrontal cortex (where executive decisions are processed). That last paragraph has made my amygdala and dorsolateral prefrontal cortex ache a bit! Basically, play is essential for sorting out how the world makes you and others feel and for making decisions about what you need to do next.

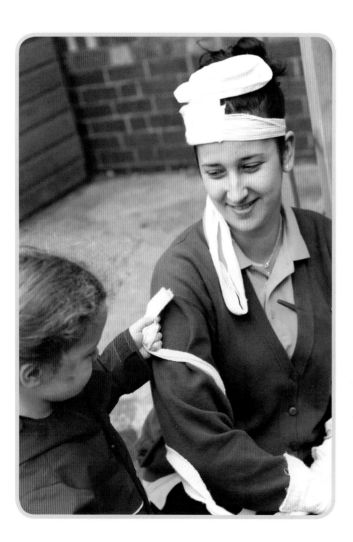

Play is a safe ground for trying and testing out life without threatening children's physical or emotional well-being. They feel safe because they know that they are playing. Even though children show a great capacity for being able to suspend their disbelief and become completely absorbed in the roles that they are playing, they still know that they are in play. Sometimes their actions step out of the realm of 'playing' (often in more physical 'superhero' play) but that is also usually a conscious decision. (See chapter 8).

For all humans, children and adults, what we play is what we know and what we experience. Sometimes our play will replicate real life, sometimes fantasy and often a mixture of both. Children can imagine possibilities, think of possible outcomes to a specific scenario and then test their thoughts. Again, role play is one of the only places where children are actively able to mix the realms of fantasy and reality, either as a solo experience or alongside others. It is the element of play that keeps them safe. It allows them to practise, imagine and rehearse problems and possibilities before they happen. Opportunities to do this will not equip children with the solutions to every eventuality they will come up against, but it will give them the strategies for problem solving and a wealth of experience to draw upon. Role playing with other children not only reinforces social interactions but gives the children involved the opportunity to learn about the thoughts, reactions and strategies of others, which will in turn enhance their own.

Successful role play

However, over–structuring and theming of role play spaces can significantly get in the way of children developing these social and emotional skills. It is difficult to expect children to be able to explore and make sense of their own personal experiences when they are being asked to do it in a Chinese restaurant or the post office! So, although theming around interest can add value to a role play experience, it should be an enhancement to your provision and not the provision in its entirety.

Instead, for a real quality role play experience, you need to provide lots of scenarios for social interaction and objects that will promote open-ended play. What is crucial is that the children have opportunities to interact and socialise, where their imaginations can run wild and take a leap – if that is what they want to do. How you have themed your role play and how you have 'dressed' your space to match will not help children to reach their full potential, it is how *well* you have provided resources, space and time that underpin the fundamental principles of role play that will stretch their imaginations.

From the day they are born, role play starts when babies mimic you as you stick out your tongue. Young children will carry on playing out your day-to-day role as you nurture and interact with them. You are part of their familiar world and they can only role play what they know – so your actions, words and routines will get centre stage! As children's knowledge of the world develops, their imagination will take on a greater role in their play and they will begin to create simulated realities that they can explore without giving up their access to the real world.

TYPES OF ROLE PLAY

We tend to see three main types of role play in children:

1. Domestic – home and family at the centre.
2. Transactional – involving goods and services and increased interaction with others.
3. Imagined world – the realms of story or places that children are unlikely to visit e.g. jungle.

> As astronauts and space travellers, children puzzle over the future; as dinosaurs and princesses they unearth the past. As weather reporters and restaurant workers they make sense of reality; as monsters and gremlins they make sense of the unreal.

Gretchen Owocki

A further necessary part of children's play and development will involve 'rough', 'superhero' or 'weapon play'. This type of play helps them to build and maintain appropriate social awareness, co-operation, fairness and altruism. It also ensures that they can distinguish between play fighting and real aggression. Role play fighting is a common feature of development the world over, both in the developed and undeveloped world. It is also a feature of role play that is shared by the majority of the animal kingdom. Contrary to popular belief it is not a precursor to violent behaviour. In fact, there is an argument that if children were given more access to play fighting then the instances of 'real' fighting would be significantly less. Still not convinced? More of this later in the book.

Good role play interacts with and involves the outside world and imagination, but fundamentally it explores the individual needs and desires of the players.

Role play provision

Thrill, will, skill

> Without thrill there is no will, and without the will, how will children successfully acquire the skill?

Alistair Bryce-Clegg

This principle applies to all aspects of early years education and the lack of it, due to over-theming, can explain why many children don't engage in the role play scenarios that we create — or if they do, their play is inconsistent with the 'theme' and therefore deemed inappropriate.

So, you may have a group of children (most likely boys) who every time the door is opened, stampede towards the outdoor area and plant themselves on a wheeled toy, or rush into your role play café and set up a robbers hide out or a den! Then, the fun really begins ... crashing, banging, hurting, destroying, fighting. You know the score. First of all, you ask nicely for more appropriate behaviour. Then you tell, nay, demand better bike etiquette, or a quieter voice. Then you threaten confiscation of the wheeled toys or compulsory eviction from the role play area until attitudes improve. The problem is ... attitudes never do, or at least not on a long-term basis. The issue isn't really about the equipment or the behaviour itself, it is more about the reason why the children behave in the way that they do.

Some of this behaviour can be attributed to how children need to make sense of the complexities of their developing world and some of that behaviour is very much about the environments that we create and the provision that we put into them. I work with lots of settings who resort to the 'throw out' or 'lock away' method. This consists of throwing the children out of the role play area or locking up the wheeled toys to 'teach children a lesson'. This is not a great solution for a number of reasons, but primarily because a lot of what the children are doing is perfectly natural and normal behaviour and finding an equally satisfying alternative to crashing their scooter into a stack of milk crates is beyond their immediate control.

There are very few children in early years, especially boys, who when their favourite thing in the world is confiscated and 'locked away' or their role play game is closed down, take time for a period of reflection, inwardly examine their misdemeanor and then vow to be better citizens! They just get grumpy and find mischief elsewhere. Part of why lots of children behave inappropriately is because they can. What they are doing is easy in terms of skill so they ramp up the risk factor which in turn increases the thrill. If you have children who are heading for the door or ignoring your role play theme, the simple fact is that there is nothing – I repeat nothing in the rest of your provision that they will find as thrilling.

> Play keeps us fit physically and mentally.

Stuart Brown

SUPPORTING LEARNING

Every area of provision that we create should have been placed there in response to a need that we have identified through assessment and observation. Our provision is there to support and extend children's learning. This could be social, it could be physical, it could be academic but it is there for a reason.

If we consider a group of children whizzing around a track at 50 miles an hour taking corners at 90 degrees, they are showing a very high level of skill and dexterity on the piece of equipment that they are using. In that respect this piece of provision is not providing challenge: the children find it easy to manipulate and that is why they like it.

If they are inventing role play scenarios that are not within the theme that you have set, that is because they are either disinterested in your theme or they don't have the language and experience to be able to access it. Therefore they resort to the play and language that is familiar to them, most often domestic (home and setting) or familiar fantasy.

Most children don't crash into each other on the bike track because they have poor co-ordination and direction skills. They crash into each other because it is fun, exciting and a little bit dangerous. They don't play fight because they actually want to hurt the other child, they do it because of the thrill of exploring and a sense of power in a safe and controlled environment. It is this thrill that gives them the will to want to engage so what we need to do is capitalise on this, and make sure that the provision on offer also develops their skill level.

POWER AND CONTROL

The other reason that children can behave in this way is their very natural desire for power and control. Although we may give them a range of choices within their everyday routines, we rarely allow them full control of what they want to do and how they want to do it. Rightly so, this is because children have not yet gained the knowledge or experience that will equip them to make this sort of decision or choice.

So, through this type of 'crash and bang' play they get the opportunity, in a controlled, safe and supportive environment, to:

- explore what is impossible and dangerous

- experience cause and effect in relation to their actions

- take 'safe' risks, which will ultimately help them to take more calculated risks in the real world

- create and explore simulated realities, without having to change what is happening in their own 'real worlds'.

ABC says

So, there is a large element of physical role play that is a perfectly normal part of children's social and emotional development that should be expected and supported rather than locked away.

THE THRILL TEST

There is also a large part of this type of play that is done purely because of the thrill factor: the thrill and the will are high but the skill is sadly lacking. For the solutions to this issue we don't need to look to child development but to our own provision. Why not give your setting a 'thrill test'?

The thrill doesn't have to come from big physical activities, it comes from any activities with high levels of engagement. Thrill can be small and quiet as well as 'Ta-Dah!'. To be able to provide a high level of thrill within your space, the one essential thing that you need is to know your children. Undoubtedly, when you discover a dinosaur bone in your digging pit, that fairies have moved into your outdoor area or an alien spaceship has crash landed outside the window, these events will promote high levels of engagement because they are 'an event'. But, although this type of event is great fun and hugely valuable, it would be very difficult (and impracticable) to have one of these every day.

Constant 'thrill' comes from identifying where children need to go next in their development and then moulding how you teach and what you teach around the interests of your children. An open-ended role play space that is enhanced with resources that respond to children's interest can give them this thrill and the desire to engage.

> Children need the freedom and time to play. Play is not a luxury. Play is a necessity.
>
> **Kay Redfield Jamison**

Familiar scenario

How many times have you seen this: a bank of computers, three boys deep. You could certainly say that you were getting the thrill and the will but this is another common example where the skill is lacking.

Now, really observe what the children are actually doing:

- Are they developing social skills and turn taking? Probably not.

- Are they taking their learning forward with programs that will extend and challenge them? Unlikely.

- Are they engaged in low-level provision thinly camouflaged as learning? Yes, probably!

- Why aren't these boys in your role play area (or anywhere else for that matter)? Because, nowhere else meets their learning desires in the same way.

We have to be careful not to confuse learning desires with learning needs. It is often easy for us to identify what a child needs to learn, where we can come unstuck as practitioners is creating a desire to learn – and that is linked to thrill, will, skill.

ABC says

What I am basically saying is that if you have gang mentality in your outdoor role play, scrums around your computers and constant confrontations in your construction while your Chinese restaurant remains void of testosterone and full of low-level domestic re-enactment, you may need to rethink.

EVALUATE YOUR PROVISION

Take some time to identify your existing areas of thrill (easy); they will indicate high levels of will; and then the harder bit: take a long hard look at the level of skill development that is taking place and then adjust the provision accordingly. We look more closely at skill levels in role play in Chapter 2, later in the book.

Although role play is the focus of this book, it is worth pointing out that this is not only about children (often, but not always, boys) on wheeled toys or in role play, it is also about children (often, but not always, girls) who will sit in mark-making or workshop areas for long periods of time and produce beautiful pieces of work. Because the work that they produce is done to such a high standard, our reaction is usually to praise them greatly for the outcome. Although this praise is essential and valid, what we should also be thinking is that if a child can produce something of this quality easily and regularly, then what else can we do within the provision, or as a result of our interactions, that will take the skill level forward?

Creative play is like a spring that bubbles up from deep within a child.

Joan Almon

Another alternative is to use high level thrill and will, but low level skill, as a mechanism for the introduction of a new skill or concept. So, even though I acknowledge that an identified group of children find whizzing around on a three-wheeled scooter very easy, so therefore the scooters are providing little in the way of challenge, I am going to use the thrill and the will that I will get from the scooters to help me to introduce these children to number, mark-making, conflict resolution … the list is truly endless.

Thrill can come from open-ended opportunities for investigation and discovery. It can also come from planned events and adult intervention. Ideally children need opportunities from a wide selection of all of the above and not just from opportunities created by an adult. There is nothing more motivating for some children than the thought that they have discovered something no-one else knew (even if an adult had planted it there in the first place!).

ABC says

Regardless of their gender, find out what thrills your children and just make sure that you use that thrill not only to ensure that they have high levels of well-being and enjoyment, but to also actively support the development of their skills. It is absolutely true, that high level engagement is the key to high level attainment but only where high level skills are employed.

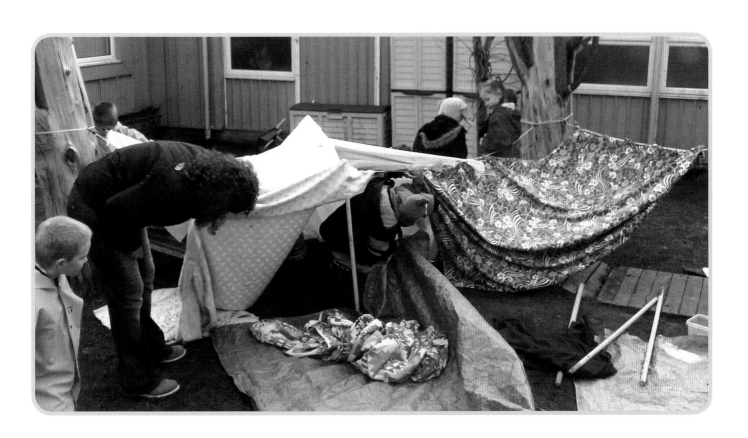

To theme, or not to theme?

That is the question! As a classroom teacher I was a great lover of themed role play as it seemed that all areas of the curriculum nestled within it, just waiting to be released by doing the same activities that I did this time last year (and probably the year before!). I showed great diligence in the creation of my 'topic map' and was chuffed at the fact that I managed to shoehorn all aspects of the teaching that I needed to do into one topic title – however tenuous the link.

My role play spaces would follow the same pattern, always prepared with a great deal of thought and effort (many weekends and holidays were lost to the creation of a cardboard café or spectacular pirate ship). It was not that I didn't put in the effort in these role play areas of magnificence, it was that I often experienced frustration at not reaping the reward of what I wanted that role play to be. Children didn't bustle into my café, to be greeted by an enthusiastic waiter who would meet them, greet them and seat them with flourish, offering them the menu and reviewing the specials of the day. This was despite the fact that each and every table was resplendent in gingham and furnished with its own wipe clean menu and fake flower in a vase. Instead, they would re-arrange the resources that had been set out. I would find menus on the floor and flowers and vases shoved into pots, pans, bags or cupboards. I seemed to spend my life constantly going into role play and berating the children for not doing it 'properly'!

When I was in there doing my 'thing' their play was always very different and far more appropriate. It didn't occur to me for a long time that the reason for this was because I was in there: I was structuring the play, giving them a scaffold of experience they didn't have and very much leading (I would probably now say, dominating) their play and learning. That was just it, my role play was not based on the interests of children nor the skills that the children needed to learn and that could be learned through that kind of play. It was driven by the need to fit into the topic. The topic was king! I am talking about 20 years ago now and you would think that things would have moved on since then, but from what I see through my work in schools and other settings, things are very much the same.

ABC says

As I have already said, high level attainment comes from high level engagement. To get maximum engagement for all children we need to have a diverse approach to the themes that we use in our teaching rather than just stick to one. Assessment will tell you what the children need to know, the hardest part is capturing their interest so that they engage in the learning process and in turn the knowledge has more chance of sticking!

Role play in continuous provision should offer children the opportunity to engage in a range of processes and create lots of possibilities for them to develop key skills. Our aim is always to get the children to master the skill or the process not to get a replicated version of pre-determined play.

More open-ended role play provision will give increased opportunities for inspiration to engender some of that mystical stuff known as 'awe and wonder'. You can enhance the play space with a huge variety of objects or experiences for the children to find or discover. Because there is no 'theme' your enhancements can be random or linked to specific interests of groups or individuals. Although you might have in your head what you think children's responses will be to the enhancements that you provide, be prepared to go with whatever they come up with, remembering that all of the children will probably not think the same.

PLAN FOR SKILL DEVELOPMENT, NOT END PRODUCT

USE CHILDREN'S INTERESTS FOR YOUR THEME

It is imperative that you are really clear that when you are planning for effective learning, you theme your teaching around children's interests not around topic or gender. Regardless of their gender you need to 'dress' your teaching around what motivates the children most. If this is dinosaurs, then provide dinosaur enhancements to your role play. If it is princesses then you must provide princess ones. This is nothing to do with 'boys' and 'girls', it is to do with interest.

If you are looking at the work of the vet, or what happens in the post office or exploring the culture of China (through a restaurant!) then add these as enhancements to your open-ended role play provision. But, and it is a big but, be prepared for children to interpret the stimulus and enhancements that you provide in very different ways from the ones that are necessarily in your head. So, if you provide a gorgeous box of Chinese restaurant resources and then some children decide to use the bowls to explore some domestic role play while being dogs, then that is alright. Don't shout out 'Oi, put those bowls down, you can only use those when you are playing Chinese restaurant!' The fact that the children are able to take something that you have introduced as a bowl for a Chinese restaurant and then reinterpret it as something else, shows a high level of imagination, creative thinking and transference. Your planning and resourcing for role play has to be flexible enough to allow this to happen, otherwise you are saying to children that there is only one way that they can interpret their learning … yours! The end product of the activities that you set up should not always lead to the same outcome. The process of creating those outcomes is the important bit. What the children explore through their play should be applied to any theme that inspires them.

ABC says

It is important to plan the skills that the children will develop but not necessarily how they will reach that point. You should therefore dress your role play for interest but not by topic. You can teach objectives, but be prepared to dress those objectives differently for different interests and you will get some high level engagement. Most of all enjoy the power, magic and individuality of children's imaginations and have some fun!

Role play skills and benefits

It used to be thought that children's dramatic play developed through similar stages to that of other forms of play:

● onlooker

● solitary

● parallel

● co-operative.

It has been shown that each of these types of play is evident at each stage of development and at some stages more of a particular style will dominate.

Play, while it cannot change the external realities of children's lives, can be a vehicle for children to explore and enjoy their differences and similarities and to create, even for a brief time, a more just world where everyone is an equal and valued participant.

Patricia G. Ramsey

IMPORTANT SKILLS

Skills that children can learn through role play include:

● **Development of pretence:** children develop the capacity to use their imagination to feed their play.

● **Development and use of receptive and expressive language:** children's ability to listen to and understand what is being said to them and also their ability to communicate their ideas and thoughts in a way that others can understand.

● **Mental representations:** ideas that children create in their mind and then play out through role play.

● **Transform objects:** children use their imagination to turn one object into another. The more ambiguous the object, the easier the process, so a box can be a boat, a house, a microwave, a shoe etc.

● **Symbolic action:** children imagine how something might 'be' or 'feel' and then use this as a mechanism for their play.

● **Interactive dialogue:** children talk to others who respond appropriately.

● **Negotiation:** children use language and conversation skills to reach a compromise or end result.

● **Role taking through choice:** children co-operate in play but decide on the role within that play that they would like to take.

● **Role taking under direction (co-operation):** children co-operate in play but are happy to be directed by another child or adult who is leading the scenario.

● **Improvisation:** children have no set or fixed plan for how their play will develop, the scenario emerges as a result of the children's interactions.

COGNITIVE STRATEGIES

- **Joint planning** – children work together to come up with a plan.

- **Negotiation** – joint discussions that lead to an agreed end result.

- **Problem solving** – taking time to think together or alone to solve a problem or issue.

- **Goal seeking** – children will work individually or in collaboration to seek an end result.

- **Emotion** – children can explore a range of emotions in a safe and supported environment.

- **Cognition** – children acquire new knowledge through language, interaction and experience.

- **Language** – children can extend their range of vocabulary as well as mechanisms for using and expressing language.

- **Sensory motor actions** – children make sense of the world through their senses and physical actions.

- **Abstract thinking** – thinking about the world around them in a different way. For productive abstract thinking, children need to be able to use and apply their prior knowledge uniquely.

- **Explicit rules** – children learn about explicit rules like playing fairly and sharing.

- **Implicit rules** – children learn about more complex and subtle rules that exist within play, such as engaging others in their play and maintaining fantasy play, even though they know that it is not 'real'.

Man is most nearly himself when he achieves the seriousness of a child at play.

Heraclitus

Role play across the Early Years Foundation Stage (EYFS)

PERSONAL, SOCIAL AND EMOTIONAL DEVELOPMENT

- co-operate, take turns and initiate role play

- develop confidence, self-esteem, self-control in re-enacting real-life situations

- learn how to work independently and access the resources they need

- learn how to work as part of a group e.g. taking on different roles in a group such as shopkeeper and customer

- express individuality and own personality through imaginative play

- use language of social interaction

- learn to have respect for others' ideas and accommodate these in role play

- help to tidy up at the end of the session

- show initiative when developing ideas in the role play area e.g. deciding to make signs for the shop

- reflect on feelings as part of role play e.g. hospital

- use role play to act out their own joys and concerns.

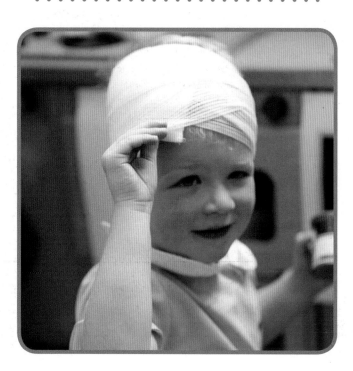

PHYSICAL DEVELOPMENT

- develop fine motor skills and co-ordination through manipulating real tools such as whisks, telephones, keyboards

- develop co-ordination through fastenings on clothes, pouring tea from teapots setting tables, dressing dolls

- develop awareness of space available in role play area and how to share that space with others.

EXPRESIVE ARTS AND DESIGN

- use imagination to develop 'stories' in the role play area

- introduce the language of colour and texture through the use of, and introduction of different types of material

- encourage children to create and design their own menus, diaries, pictures, price lists, posters, leaflets, cards

- make items for role play e.g. playdough, buns, cakes, biscuits for shop, junk materials for sandwiches, burgers, meals for café.

UNDERSTANDING THE WORLD

- create role play areas based on knowledge about their local environment
- talk about their families in relation to events in role play
- re-enact special occasions e.g. wedding, birthday party, Christmas
- relate the work of people in the local community to role play e.g. visits within the local community: fire station, farm, local shops
- explore and recognise features of living things e.g. through hospital, vets, garden centre role play
- explore and recognise feature of how things work through garage or toy shop role play
- explore and select materials and equipment appropriate to the role play
- develop scientific skills, knowledge and concepts through role play – topics may include babies, holes, wheels.

- use technology e.g. a shopping till, calculator
- select appropriate materials to make models e.g. wheeled vehicles, prams, furniture etc., for use in role play area
- develop skills of cutting, folding, joining.

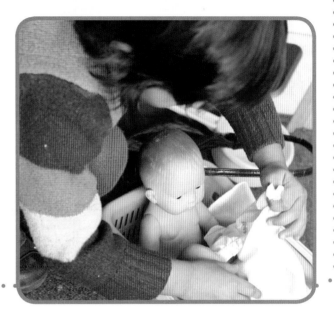

COMMUNICATION AND LANGUAGE

- talk about what different people do in role play situations
- talk in the language of different roles e.g. shopkeeper, mummy, Little Red Riding Hood
- role play nursery rhymes, stories
- use language to plan and create real-life or imaginary situations
- develop the language of dialogue e.g. listen to and respond to what other children/adults say
- extend vocabulary associated with imaginary/role play e.g. hospital, airport, artists studio, garden centre
- have access to related books fact/fiction in role play area
- develop writing skills e.g. writing shopping lists, prescriptions, Get Well cards, record sheets, forms, bills, leaflets, menus, letters
- develop ICT skills through office role play: telephones, keyboards, photocopier, computer.

MATHEMATICS

- explore various mathematical concepts related to money, capacity, size, weight, one-to-one correspondence
- use language related to all of the above e.g. how much, full, empty, need more/less, heavy, light
- problem solve through imaginative play e.g. How much money will I need for this item? How many cups will I need for the family?
- develop concept of time in house play: breakfast, dinner, bedtime, time in doctor's surgery, refer to clocks, watches
- order, sort, match in role play area.

Whoever wants to understand much must play much.

Gottfried Benn

Benefits of role play

> Effective role play ensures 'children can try out risky ideas in a safe universe. They can explore boundaries, make sense of their world and develop their own identity. Children are also really exploring concepts that are very important to understand: good and bad, win and lose, boy and girl and the family.'
>
> **Anne Flemmert**

Role play is important to a child's development, as it is through this type of play that they begin to understand very fundamental principles of our society and how it actually functions; what the rules and routines of traditional behaviour are. Then, after that, they can start making their universes much more complex. What does it mean to be a farmer/nurse? What kind of roles are they? When they are role playing being a doctor, a great deal of their play will be based on their own first-hand experience. Their play will be limited to the role that they perceive that the person they are playing does. Children also get great benefits from having the opportunity to explore fantasy through role play. However, in fantasy role play there are no such boundaries: anything can happen because it is fantasy!

ABC says

Role play is vital because it supports the child's imagination and allows them to think 'what if?'; to be able to imagine other worlds than the one we inhabit at this moment, which actually helps us change the things we are not happy with, and makes us do things which we wouldn't have done if we didn't have that imaginative side.

DEVELOPING SKILLS

Role play in our settings has many benefits and helps children to develop a range of skills:

Empathy: This is one of the hardest skills for some young children to master as it is very difficult to put yourself in someone else's shoes when your own shoes don't quite fit yet! I will go on to talk more in this chapter and throughout the book about how crucial the development of empathy is and how you can use role play to facilitate it.

Real language experiences: Good role play activities provide children with the opportunity to communicate in authentic ways and situations. This helps them to revisit and rehearse many of the day-to-day situations that they will have come up against in their everyday lives.

Extended language experiences: Role play can be used really effectively to extend children's vocabulary and language use. The key to success here is the role of the other adult (or in some cases, peer). When children are engaged in an exciting role play experience, they can only use the language that they know already, new language is not going to spring into their head like magic. So engaging role play scenarios are essential to 'hook' the children in but the role of the adult is crucial in recognising the language mechanisms and the vocabulary that children are using and then sharing. This is new and exciting language that will take that learning forward.

Memorable learning experience: This is regardless of whether children are using role play to consolidate a home life experience, a fantasy experience or something linked to learning you have facilitated in your setting. The high levels of willing engagement that you get for a well planned role play will usually ensure that some high level attainment takes place. If your role play provision is good then children will want to return to it again and again (as will the adults).

Adaptability: If you want children to be able to experience, consolidate and then practise all of the skills that a good role play area can offer then 'adaptability' is the key. If you are over themed or over prescriptive in your role play theme then you are significantly reducing learning opportunities. What motivates one child in their play does not always motivate another. So why would 30 children all be motivated by the same thing?

> Play is the only way the highest intelligence of humankind can unfold.

Joseph Chilton Pearce

Builds confidence: Role play allows children to explore different ideas, project themselves in different ways and get involved in group or team play. All of these things help to raise their confidence and self esteem.

Language fluency: Practising dialogue, using realistic scenarios and role playing will enable children to become more fluent with their own language and experience the language of others. Using role play will allow them to practise words, phrases, and sentences in a realistic setting.

Spontaneity: Much of group role play, by its very nature, involves making it up as you go along. As there is no prescribed pathway or script, children have more opportunity for spontaneity and this often also has an impact on their creativity where they have complete freedom to do and say whatever comes into their heads.

Assessment: There are a huge number of opportunities for assessement by observing children in role play, from the more obvious and apparent assessment of vocabulary and language structure to the more subtle aspects of child development such as confidence and schema.

Exploring culture: For children with English as an Additional Language, engaging in role play with other children allows them to experience language in context and reinforces the labeling of familiar objects. Enhancing our role play areas (rather than over-theming them) with resources from other cultures is a really effective way to introduce children to cultural similarities and differences in a tangible way.

Aspects of role play development

Two important areas of development in role play involve the 'Theory of Mind' and private speech, where children self-coach during play.

Theory of Mind

'Theory of Mind' (ToM) is the ability to understand that others have thoughts and feeling all of their own. Young children are very aware of their own thoughts at feelings but often show little or no recognition that others may be experiencing similar emotions. In the first few years of life, children are egocentric: they think the world does indeed revolve around them and their primary concern is themselves. But to be fair, that is how nature has made us. When we were babies and were hungry, someone fed us; when we fell over, someone picked us up; when we cried, someone cuddled us; so why would we think that life was ever going to be any different? At this age and stage, a baby has not developed to a point where they can look past their own needs and consider the needs of others.

Usually around the age of three or four children begin to develop an ability to start to recognise their own feelings and, as a next step on from there, are able to imagine that someone else might be feeling the same. Once you can recognise the way you have felt in someone else, then you are more likely to make an appropriate response to that person. Children are therefore developing a ToM. In short, they have a theory (idea) about what someone else is feeling, based on their recognition of their own feelings. As adults we are able to make these assumptions easily, without even thinking that we are doing something quite amazing. We spend most of our time, when we are socially interacting with other people, making predictions about what is going on in their heads and, amazingly, these predictions most often are right.

> Creative people are curious, flexible, persistent, and independent with a tremendous spirit of adventure and a love of play.
>
> **Henri Matisse**

One of the most important milestones in theory of mind development is gaining the ability to 'attribute false belief'; this means to recognise that other people can believe something that you know to be wrong. To do this, children need to understand that what you believe comes from what you know.

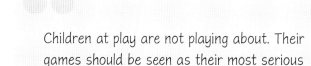

Children at play are not playing about. Their games should be seen as their most serious minded activity.

Michel de Montaigne

FALSE BELIEF TESTS

The most famous test for false belief was carried out by Wimmer and Perner (1983).

The Sally Anne test

In the experiment, children are told or shown a story involving two characters. In one version, the child is shown two dolls, Sally and Anne, playing with a marble. The dolls put away the marble in a box and then Sally leaves. Anne takes the marble out and plays with it again, but after she has finished she puts it away in a different box. Sally returns and the child is then asked where Sally will look for the marble.

The crucial point is, will the child use their immediate knowledge of where the marble is now or will they understand that Sally didn't see the marble move, therefore she still thinks it is in the first box? The child passes the task if they answer that Sally will look in the first box where she put the marble.

Smarties

In another test, a child was shown a tube of Smarties and asked what they thought was in the tube. Of course, as any self respecting child would, they answered 'Smarties'. When the tube was opened, the child could see that there weren't Smarties inside, there were in fact pencils (what a disappointment!). The child was then asked what their friend would think might be in the tube. Again, the child passes the test if they say 'Smarties'.

As an interesting addition to this test, one group of children were asked what their friend would think was in the tube and then the friend was called over and asked. When the first child was then asked 'Can you remind me what you said when I asked you that question?' Many answered 'pencils'. Even though they knew it was a lie!

This can be a difficult (and long) stage of development for some children, but it is perfectly natural for them not to recognise or empathise with the needs of others. As a result, we should expect this sort of behaviour and work with children to raise their awareness of the feeling of others. Role play is a great mechanism for this.

One of the most common issues that pre-school settings have is the inability of children to share. The question I always ask is 'Why would you want to share?' If you had something that you want why would you give it up just because someone else wants it?

Part of the reason that children do learn to share is that they develop ToM. They understand how the other child is feeling and that awareness prompts them to alter their own behaviour. ToM doesn't just allow us to predict what someone else is thinking, it is also a fundamental skill in our ability to be compassionate, keep a secret, tell a lie, and be sarcastic!

USING ROLE PLAY

Role play can offer some fantastic opportunities for children to explore familiar scenarios, not just from their own point of view, but from the point of view of others. This in turn helps them to begin to develop their own sense of ToM. From studies of imaginary friends to those examining when and how well children distinguish reality from fantasy, researchers are developing theories about the role of imagination and pretend play in child development.

Even though children don't develop a sophisticated ToM until somewhere between three and five years old, it would seem that they need to understand something about others' thoughts and feelings if they are to begin pretending themselves.

If I climb into a cardboard box and pretend to turn on the engine and steer around corners, a child playing alongside me must begin to realise that I am projecting my idea of a car onto a cardboard box. I am sharing an abstract thought with that child and they get it! In this situation that child is probably not recognising my emotions, just sharing in the fact that I am using my imagination. When the child begins to enhance our play with emotion then they are showing the development of ToM.

Children's role play suggests that they can enact what people might do in a given situation because they imagine themselves in that same situation and act in an appropriate way. In the same way, when a child faces a real-life situation, he or she can use the same process to predict how another person might react. If a child has the opportunity to play out and rehearse a wide variety of social interactions through role play they can practise possible outcomes in a safe and secure way. This will greatly support their ability to respond appropriately in a real situation where you only get one opportunity to give a reaction to that situation and you don't have the privilege to be able to say 'Can we play that again and this time …'.

ABC says

The key here, as with most aspects of role play development, is that the opportunities that you create for children's role play have to be diverse and open-ended. The more themed and structured your role play provision, the less opportunities children get to explore and rehearse the life that is real to them.

Private speech: self coaching in role play

Private speech is another feature of children's early role play development. As children become more self aware, and their play begins to increasingly engage with other children, their private speech becomes less evident and often disappears completely.

So, what is private speech? Well, it came to promimence primarily through the work of Vygotsky and Piaget and is most evident in children from the age of two to seven. It is literally where children will talk to themselves during play and although this talk is audible, it is not directed at anyone else. It is like an internal dialogue where children coach themselves through an activity or situation. A strong correlation has been found between children who use a high level of private talk and the achievement of success in the task in which they are engaged. Children have been found to use more private talk when they are highly engaged and when they are involved in an activity with a goal at the end that they really want to achieve.

As an adult observing children in their play, you can find out a great deal of information about that child through their private speech. Not only the level of the language that they use, but also what challenges, motivates and inspires them. This knowledge is invaluable when you are planning how you can support that child further in their learning. During role play children will often use private speech almost as an ongoing discussion with themselves about what the characters in their play might be thinking or feeling or what they are going to do next. The more children engage in private speech during role play, often the more creative and imaginative their play. This is because they are not acting on the first impulse, idea or solution, but are taking time to think and find alternative solutions.

> Necessity may be the mother of invention, but play is certainly the father.

Roger von Oech

HOW CAN WELL PLANNED ROLE PLAY BENEFIT CHILDREN?

The benefits to children's development of role play is extensive. In short: it helps children to make sense of their world.

- Children can learn many skills and attitudes.

- Good role play encourages co-operation and conflict resolution.

- It allows children to take risks in an imaginary and safe environment.

- It can give children a sense of power and control that they do not get in their own life.

- It allows children to make decisions and act upon them, therefore experiencing the positives and negatives of cause and effect.

- It encourages individual and co-operative play.

- Long periods in role play give children opportunities to use repetition in the content of their play choices to find resolution.

- Children can learn to empathise with others.

- They can learn about other cultures.

- It gives children opportunities to express feelings.

- It can help develop language and literacy.

- It can provide many opportunities to develop understanding of mathematical concepts and problem solving skills.

- The creation and use of role play spaces also impacts on children's gross and fine motor skills.

- Role play encourages abstract thinking, sustained shared thinking and creates many opportunities for deep level learning.

Chapter 4

Stages of role play development

What children chose to role play and how they chose to do it is very closely linked to their stage of development and first-hand experience. The following statements are based on the type of play that is 'usually' seen with this age group. However, as role play is so closely linked to experience, it is more important to consider the stage of overall development rather than their age.

Birth to two years old

Even from the day that they are born, babies have the amazing ability to imitate. They will watch you intently as you stick out your tongue and then, as if they have been practising for ever – do the same right back at you. This ability and desire to imitate is part of our human nature. In only a few months children will begin to imitate the facial expressions, speech patterns and mannerisms of the people that are familiar to them and represent them in their play.

As human beings we also have well-developed memories that enable us to remember a lot of what we see, feel, and hear. So, a great deal of what children experience in their very early stages of development will stay with them and help to lay the groundwork for the imaginative pretend play of the toddler years.

In some cases, these memories might be ones of warmth and nurture, but sadly not in all. That is why it is important that we try to understand how and why a child plays in the way that they do and make sure that we create role play spaces that allow children to explore, rehearse and work through their thoughts, feelings and emotions.

REAL AND SYMBOLIC

By the age of 12 to 14 months, most toddlers begin to use toys in specific and appropriate ways, they become familiar with what they are and what they do. A child of this age will know that a ball is for throwing and a pram is for pushing. Within the next six months, symbolic play is likely to begin, and the child might start to substitute symbolic items for real toys using a car as a brick, a peg, a doll. Children will also begin to use symbolic items to support their play, such as using boxes to build a garage for their car, or leaves for plates in their outdoor café.

Around two years old, when most children are beginning to develop some language, you will see them using toys and other 'props' to re-enact a familiar task or experience: they might pick up a bag to go to the shops or use a toy car to re-enact their journey to their setting. As this sort of familiar re-enactment play still forms the majority of children's role play experience, it is important that we stock our role play areas with resources to support and extend what children know and are familiar with.

FANTASY AND DRAMA

Around the age of two, children begin to engage in more simple dramatic play. Not only are their language skills increasing, they also have a greater awareness of the world around them. If children also have ample access to stories and other fantasy experiences they will store what they have learned and then channel it through their own play – however crude their version.

A toddlers' grasp of the line between fantasy and reality, however, can still be very fragile. I told my two year old niece that there was a crocodile coming to get us as part of our game the other day and she cried. She asks about the crocodile every time she comes to our house. I hope I don't end up with therapy bills in years to come!

NURTURED IMAGINATION

It is important at this stage of development that we help children to explore their familiar play, while feeding their imagination with experiences that will support their imaginative and fantasy play. At this stage of development children are often very free in their play. They do not have a high level of awareness of social stereotyping and expectations. We need to encourage them in this freedom, giving them lots of opportunities to explore, create and revisit play that makes them feel secure. It is by having a good foundation of familiar play experience that they will be well equipped to engage in the more creative and fantastical.

THE ADULT'S ROLE

Adults play a crucial role in helping young children to expand their ability to role play. The spaces that we create to support role play need to be considered and linked to the current stage of a child's development. The resources that we offer need to be a combination of real and familiar, as well as open-ended and ambiguous. We need to play with children to support their real experiences while also modelling the concept of substituting 'real' resources with imagination.

As with every aspect of early years practice the right level of adult intervention is a real skill. Getting it right isn't always obvious or easy: often we can intervene too strongly or too often and end up 'railroading' any play that is taking place.

DEVELOPING EARLY ROLE PLAY

Give babies a variety of toys: instruments, toys that roll, toys that can change shape, wooden blocks to bang. Opportunities to explore familiar toys and everyday objects can be the first step towards symbolic play as children begin to learn that an object can be or do more than one thing, depending on how you use it.

When symbolic play begins, provide toys with a purpose. It is important to be aware of what is 'familiar' to a child in their everyday life. When they have been involved in festivals or celebrations for example, they may want to re-enact key elements of their experience so the resources that we provide for role play should reflect this. Expand play by modeling experiences: if a child is role playing making cakes with dough, you could ask if the cakes are for someone's birthday or a tea party and help the play to take a new direction.

Eighteen months to two years:
the beginnings of pretend play

During this stage of their development, children will begin to translate their everyday world into single actions that they will then offer to another person or a toy. They might hold a cup up towards someone's mouth or a phone to their ear. It is around now that children begin to substitute a toy object for the real thing, although at this stage the things need to look very similar. Miniature versions of real objects are useful for specific play.

THE ADULT'S ROLE

Children's role play involves a great deal of mimicry of adults in familiar situations like reading the paper, washing the dishes or serving the snack, so your role is crucial in providing useful, meaningful examples of behaviour.

Two to two and a half years old:
the beginnings of role play

Around about now children will begin to play out a sequence of several pretend actions in the correct order, such as getting dressed and having their breakfast or their bedtime routine. In these re-enactments children also often begin to take on the role of another person (usually a significant adult) and this process can begin with the language or actions that that person may use. If a child is role playing brushing their teeth they might say 'Well done (name)' when they have finished: they are being themselves and the other adult in their role play at the same time!

As this sort of play continues, the roles that they are playing will become more apparent and separated until the child might choose to play one role or the other while interacting with another adult or child. Children will also begin to substitute their toys into familiar roles like making them tea, putting them to bed and bathing them.

Two and a half to three years old:
less familiar events

At this age children can start role playing less familiar events and may use ambiguous objects for a specific purpose. They may begin to draw upon their knowledge of less familiar events in their life for their role play, like a visit to the hairdresser or the dentist.

Their role play tends to be more action based and doesn't necessarily involve a great deal of talk or interaction with others.

If they have had lots of experience of naming and experiencing first-hand objects, children will begin to use their imaginations to pretend with objects that don't look like the real thing — so a box might become a shop till, and a wooden block a train. Usually around this time you would also begin to see the development of imaginary objects that have no concrete physical form. This imaginative play will become more prevalent between the ages of three and four, where the existence of the 'imaginary friend' is most often seen.

Three to four years:
socio-dramatic play

This stage introduces dramatic play with the additional component of social interaction.

Children's role play is beginning to become more sophisticated: it is more about social interaction than it is about objects that they are familiar with. It is around now that children really begin to 'role play' in the truest sense of the phrase, as they will be taking on the roles of others, both real and imagined. There are lots of opportunities at this stage to work with children on the concept of empathy and conflict resolution.

There are six key aspects to socio-dramatic play:

1. Role play
2. Interaction with one or more children or adults
3. Playing for longer periods
4. Lots of talk interaction, based around the play
5. Use of make believe instead of real objects
6. Use of language to describe the make believe actions or settings

It's for my friend. He's invisible!

OTHER KEY DEVELOPMENTS AT THIS AGE

As I have already said, the age of three is often the time when an extra guest moves into your house or setting for a while: you will have to leave them a space at the table, help to get them dressed, make sure they can see the television and wait while their every word is interpreted through your child. This is an important stage of development for some children, but not all. Of my three sons only the eldest had an imaginary friend, who I distinctly remember arriving, but can't remember going! I think he eventually just got phased out in my son's head and therefore phased out of our lives. (Thank goodness, as imaginary friends go he was high maintenance!) Three-year-olds will begin to experiment with acting out lots of roles, often simultaneously. They will change their characters and their story lines in quick succession. It is important therefore that our role play opportunities are not over themed to allow this change to happen easily.

Four years:
getting real

Around four years of age is when children's play becomes more complex and more real. Children will take a simple premise for play like a birthday party or a fire and expand it with their own real experience and some imagination. The use of language is greater, the social interaction increases and there is significantly more detail than there has been in the context of their play. Lots of the content of a four year olds play will based in fantasy, but by this age the children have usually got a clear idea of the difference between reality and make believe. When they shoot each other in a battle and die, they know that that no one is really dead and that they will all be able to get up and fight another day!

IS IT A BIRD? IS IT A PLANE?

No, it is often very loud, often very physical, often boy-dominated, often misunderstood — superhero play. This sort of play is a very normal part of children's development and allows them to explore feelings of safety, risk and power in a safe and secure environment. When supported well, it also provides lots of opportunities to take learning into an area of high level engagement. I will look at this aspect of role play in more detail in Chapter 8 'Superhero and weapon play'.

THE ADULT'S ROLE

At three and four years old, children are making sense of the world that they are experiencing, especially in relation to social interactions and re-enactment of first-hand experiences. We need to provide lots of different familiar role experiences for children to rehearse and revisit, and we need to give children plenty of familiar cultural props to support their play and use of familiar language. We should offer resources that reflect the familiar experiences that the children have talked about or that we have observed them trying to recreate in their play.

Alongside these familiar props we also need to provide more open-ended opportunities for children to use their imagination and prior knowledge and be creative in their play. Providing open-ended resources such as boxes and pieces of fabric can really help to extend their learning.

Using familiar stories and rhymes as a prompt for role play can be particularly effective at this stage of development. Choose stories that children like and know well and provide opportunities for them to recreate the story in role play. Don't restrict this to just your role play area, extend the children's role playing skills through other areas like small world and puppets both indoors and out.

Four and five years old:
inventive and imaginative play

Role play becomes more sophisticated and complex at this stage of children's development. They have had more experience of the world around them, so have more knowledge to draw on. The content of children's play is still very much centered on basic relationships and interactions, but the setting for that play and the complexity of the storyline and character often becomes much richer. Children may use non-specific resources, adapting them for their play situation as required.

Rather than a high element of solo play or re-enactment of a familiar story or situation, children use more language of co-operation and work together to create a scenario or solve a problem. Although the play is often led by one or two children who will 'direct', you will see a greater prevalence of group play and willing co-operation. Children will be able to role play for much longer periods of time and ideally need to be provided with extended opportunities for role play to allow them to follow through their ideas and rehearse and revisit the different scenarios that they have created.

To help this to happen we should also be prepared to let the role play move out of the designated role play space. As children move more and more away from needing familiar objects to role play with, they open up greater opportunities to explore their play throughout the entire environment.

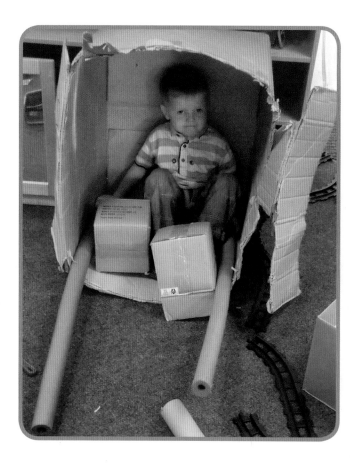

THE ADULT'S ROLE

Be a good role model and play partner. In any setting there will be children at different stages of their role play development and some children will need an adult to help them to extend their play with possible ideas and scenarios. Others will require your help to enable them to facilitate their ideas by providing resources, time and space. It is important that children see adults who engage with and value their play.

Provide a range of stimulating experiences, always remembering that children can only role play what they know, so if they have little experience of something their role play capabilities will be limited. We can provide real experiences in the form of trips or visitors to the setting, but it is important that we also provide lots of other stimuli such as books, stories, films and resources that children can use to support and enhance their chosen play theme.

Five and beyond!

I'm ready for my close up!

Reception age children usually have a strong compulsion to play and pretend. They can slip in and out of characters with ease and clarity. Throughout the early years children develop a thorough understanding of the difference between real and pretend and come to understand when a story or character is real life and when it is fantasy. This awareness of self and others is an important building block for their fantasy play. They can really experiment with creating wild and wonderful scenarios while still being very secure in who they are.

At this stage we will see children's play themes last for a whole day, and often longer. Popular play scenarios will run both indoors and out and can dominate children's play choices for long periods of time. The themes for this sort of play can also be very random. Recently I was working with a setting where a large group of children had been playing 'meatball firing plant' game for over a week. Seemingly the world was being taken over by gigantic plants that fired spicy meatballs. Although the actual play was typical superhero/weapon play the context was high level fantasy. At this stage children's increased attention span and awareness of details enable them to modify and embellish plots as they return to them each day, picking up where they left off.

WORKING TOGETHER

Five year olds apply their developing social skills to their pretending. When younger children play we see a definite pattern of children working on their own, replaying their own experiences or creating role play scenarios with characters and situations that are very specific to them. As children get older, they prefer to be part of a company of actors. Part of the fun is interacting with one another – discussing roles, sharing ideas for props, trying out different lines.

THE ADULT'S ROLE

You can encourage children's play to come out of the role play area and into every other area of learning. Children usually love to role play and you can use this high level of engagement to get some high level attainment. Children need extended opportunities for free role play to explore their own thought and concepts, but as adults we can also utilise the power of role play through adult-led interactions, where we deliver key learning objectives as well as having some fun.

Share a good book: Children learn a huge amount about real life, fantasy, language and story through good books. It is really important to share as many books as you can with your children but also to make key props (and the book itself) available for role play. There is no need to completely resource your role play for every book that you read. Apart from being impractical, children at this stage of development will be quite happy to substitute real objects with imaginary or substitute resources.

Make your mark: Provide lots of opportunities to mark-make as part of role play. Don't just get the children to make shopping lists and appointments, provide them with large pieces of blank paper to create drawings to enhance their role play, link your 'Creative' area with your role play so that children can create their own props and costumes using the skills that they have learned through creativity.

Keep it real: Use your role play and small world areas to support children in solving real issues that might arise from their social interactions. It is hard for young children to come up with solutions to personal and social issues in the heat of the moment. Being able to explore the same issue as a different character in a safe scenario can have really successful results.

Things to think about in your role play area

- Do the children have opportunities to organise and re-organise the role play resources?

- Do you involve children and value their thoughts and ideas when planning a new role play area?

- Do you plan the role play according to their own interests and stages of development rather than an adult generated theme that fits with your topic?

- Do the children have easy access to a variety of real and open-ended items?

- Is there a wide selection of dressing-up clothes that reflect different roles, cultures and genders?

- Do you have a collection of different fabrics for the children to clip, tie, fix to static equipment and do you encourage children to make their own costumes and props for their play?

- Are there always opportunities for mark-making?

- Do you encourage children to link role play to other areas of your space?

> "The true object of all human life is play."
>
> G. K. Chesterton

Quick reminder

BIRTH TO TWO

- Children will use their immediate and direct experience to prompt what they re-enact in their play.

- In their second year, children begin to engage in symbolic play so a doll will represent a baby, and blocks will become a garage or a house.

- More imaginative fantasy gradually emerges in the pretend play of two-year-olds.

- Two-year-olds sometimes lose sight of the line between fantasy and reality – even in their own pretending.

THREE TO FOUR

- Around the age of three, play is often related to children's real-life experiences. It will usually involve interaction with others and often includes props and lots of language.

- In the early stages of peer play, one child often assigns roles to the others who may find creative ways to make up their own play.

- Imaginary friends often appear when children are around the age of three.

- Four year olds' role play often becomes more sophisticated and will contain a lot of reference to detail.

FIVE TO SIX

- Children at this age have a strong grasp of the difference between real and pretend. As a result of this you will often see a greater prevalence of more complex fantasy play.

- Because the play at this age is often more complex and involved, children will usually stick at it for longer periods of time.

- A great deal of play will be based around exploring and rehearsing social interaction in a variety of scenarios.

Stages of role play and stages of talk

Role play usually follows the same stages of development as language acquisition which makes sense, as children need a certain level of language to be able to articulate the content and complexity of what they want to play. When language development is not supported, children's role play can stagnate and remain centred on their own personal experience and not involve a high level of social interaction. As practitioners, it is essential that we are aware of the development of children's talk and how we can support this through play.

When children are in role play, the first thing they decide on is the role that they are going to play. In the early stages of play this is often a very familiar role and then as their play develops that role becomes more abstract. Even if the children decide to be themselves they are still playing a 'role' in an imagined or reinterpreted scenario. Next comes the scenario. Once they have decided who they are going to be then they will create an event or series of events to play out. Again this starts out with the familiar and moves on towards the more abstract. The last key component in role play is the props or objects that children use to facilitate their play. Sometimes these are actual objects that are fulfilling this role in a very real sense. Sometimes they are objects that the children interpret as something else, and sometimes they are invisible. Even though there is no actual, tangible object there, the child is still creating an image of that object in their head and through their play.

How role play develops

STAGE 1

Children play only with realistic toys and show no interest in object substitution performed by adults.

Children at this stage demonstrate a very early realisation that they can 'pretend'. Through play they can create familiar actions and scenarios that they are revisiting based on their experiences. In this initial stage of play, children tend to act, talk, and dress like people they know and they will use real objects as props in their play. There is a high, almost exclusive element of reality in their play. For instance, a child may pick up a spoon and pretend to feed a doll or teddy bear; they may pick up a phone and mimic talking to their mother or father. Children start to develop a concept of a 'pretended role' but need to ground that with the actual props that are used. This play is most often a solitary activity.

STAGE 2

Children automatically imitate adult-initiated object substitutions, but do not appear to understand that one object has been substituted for another. For example, an adult uses a banana as a phone, the child copies the action in play with the adults.

In this second stage, children's play is enhanced by their developing imaginations. They are now less dependent on concrete props for role playing and they may use a box as a car, or a basket as a hat. The ability to make believe moves beyond the scope of real props or costumes and children also learn to use their imaginations to invent actions and situations. At this stage of development we also begin to see the emergence of fantasy that takes the children's play outside of their real-life experiences. At this stage, children often use such play to help them understand feelings or deal with fears and worries.

STAGE 3

Children independently imitate object
substitutions previously performed by an adult.
For example, an adult uses a banana as a phone,
the child copies the action in independent play.

During this stage of development, socio-dramatic play
emerges with children beginning to seek out and enjoy the
interaction of playing with others. As more children become
involved in the play then it becomes more complex and
lasts for longer periods of time. This sort of play includes
elements of real-life play and make believe play and unlike
the aspects of this sort of play that we have seen in earlier
children's development, this requires social interaction and
the contribution of two children or more. Because of its
interactive nature, this sort of play requires planning and
often the planning can take up as much time as the playing.
Because of its more complex story lines, socio-dramatic play
requires that children spend a significant amount of time in
this type of play.

STAGE 4

Children select their own substitute objects,
but do not rename the objects with substitute
names. For example, a child independently selects
a wooden brick as a substitute for a phone.

Here the child may act out the different roles played by real
and fantasy characters that they are familiar with. Unlike
a 'play' they will not stick to one role but move between a
number of them, shaping the story as they go (very clever!).
Through this sort of play children can explore the emotions of
different characters and also experience an element of power
as they shape the outcomes of their story. The children
would normally imitate adult roles and also play alongside
adults to expand their experiences.

STAGE 5

> Children create unique and fantastical play scenarios.

Here role playing with peers is paramount and fantasy is often a key element of play and children will put themselves into completely fantastic roles like that of an alien or mermaid. You will also see them invent unique fantasy beings and creatures from their own imagination based on all the knowledge and experience they have amassed. For children who display more advanced role play skills, they will move on from playing a generic role like 'a nurse' or 'shopkeeper', to assuming the character of people that they know copying their familiar language, speech patterns, intonation and mannerisms.

The creation of something new is not accomplished by the intellect but by the play instinct.

Carl Jung

In play a child always behaves beyond his average age, above his daily behavior. In play it is as though he were a head taller than himself.

Lev Vygotsky

How talk develops

If you refer to the age-related descriptors for Communication and Language in the EYFS, they provide a very comprehensive reference point, not only for the type of talk activity that you should be planning, but also the national expectation for age-related attainment.

SKILLS FOR TALK DEVELOPMENT

22–36 months

* Uses language as a powerful means of widening contacts, sharing feelings, experiences and thoughts.

* Holds a conversation, jumping from topic to topic.

* Learns new words very rapidly and is able to use them in communicating.

* Uses gestures, sometimes with limited talk, e.g. reaches toward toy, saying 'I have it'.

* Uses a variety of questions (e.g. what, where, who).

* Uses simple sentences (e.g. 'Mummy gonna work').

* Beginning to use word endings (e.g. going, cats).

30–50 months

* Beginning to use more complex sentences to link thoughts (e.g. using and, because).

* Can retell a simple past event in correct order (e.g. went down slide, hurt finger).

* Uses talk to connect ideas, explain what is happening and anticipate what might happen next, recall and relive past experiences.

* Questions why things happen and gives explanations. Asks e.g. who, what, when, how.

* Uses a range of tenses (e.g. play, playing, will play, played).

* Uses intonation, rhythm and phrasing to make the meaning clear to others.

* Uses vocabulary focused on objects and people that are of particular importance to them.

* Builds up vocabulary that reflects the breadth of their experiences.

* Uses talk in pretending that objects stand for something else in play, e.g. 'This box is my castle.'

40–60+ months

* Extends vocabulary, especially by grouping and naming, exploring the meaning and sounds of new words.

* Uses language to imagine and recreate roles and experiences in play situations.

* Links statements and sticks to a main theme or intention.

* Uses talk to organise, sequence and clarify thinking, ideas, feelings and events.

* Introduces a storyline or narrative into their play.

Early Learning Goal

Children express themselves effectively, showing awareness of listeners' needs. They use past, present and future forms accurately when talking about events that have happened or are to happen in the future. They develop their own narratives and explanations by connecting ideas or events.

The range of talk skills that children are able to develop are quite diverse and complex. Far in advance of what they are expected to record in their writing.

SKILLS FOR WRITING DEVELOPMENT

* Distinguishes between the different marks they make.

* Sometimes gives meaning to marks as they draw and paint.

* Ascribes meanings to marks that they see in different places.

* Gives meaning to marks they make as they draw, write and paint.

* Begins to break the flow of speech into words.

* Continues a rhyming string.

* Hears and says the initial sound in words.

* Can segment the sounds in simple words and blend them together.

* Links sounds to letters, naming and sounding the letters of the alphabet.

* Uses some clearly identifiable letters to communicate meaning, representing some sounds correctly and in sequence.

* Writes own name and other things such as labels, captions.

* Attempts to write short sentences in meaningful contexts.

Early Learning Goal

Children use their phonic knowledge to write words in ways which match their spoken sounds. They also write some irregular common words. They write simple sentences which can be read by themselves and others. Some words are spelt correctly and others are phonetically plausible.

These lists are really useful reference for looking at what 'next steps' for talk might look like in your planning, but also for mapping how you can support children and their talk and mark making through role play.

Creating an effective role play space

Ideas for successful role play include providing a range of materials and props to enable children to create their own role play spaces, using small world toys to create role play scenarios and using traditional tales to inspire role play ideas.

Deconstructed role play

By far the best mechanism I have ever used to accomplish successful role play is to create a deconstructed role play space that has a good balance of child-led and adult-initiated role play. To run a deconstructed role play area, the children you are working with have to be old enough to be familiar with lots of aspects of day-to-day life. A good deconstructed role play area needs to be big enough to get a few children in it. If you have identified language and personal skills as key for development then they need to be represented in a large portion of your environment. If your role play is one small corner which becomes packed with three children in it, then it's unlikely to have any significant impact.

You are going to fill your identified space with ... well, anything! By that I mean things like: cardboard boxes, large sheets, crates, bread trays – the list is endless. You are aiming to create a role play space that can change continually depending on who is in it: a café is a café until you change it into the vet's; a pile of boxes can also be a café and ten minutes later a vet's and then a submarine and then 'my granny's house'. It is this level of versatility that not only challenges children to use their imaginations but also offers high-level engagement.

I often take out all of the costumes and replace them with pieces of fabric – again this encourages children to really use their imagination and creativity. There is also no display in my deconstructed role play: the walls are backed in plain paper

> It is in playing, and only in playing, that the individual child or adult is able to be creative and to use the whole personality, and it is only in being creative that the individual discovers the self.
>
> **D.W. Winnicott**

and the children are encouraged to draw a backdrop that suits their play. Don't expect them to produce something like a theatre set! You will often get a series of small drawings and marks, which the children then play to.

As I have already mentioned traditional role play is very adult directed and can be over-themed. We might set up a shop, pirate ship or the vet's in our role play area. When there is an adult leading the play, using the language, acting out scenarios then the children can easily access the experience: the adult facilitates their play. But when there is no adult the children have to rely on their own life experience to provide them with the tools that they need to be able to play in that particular environment. How many of the children that we work with have ever been in the operating theatre of a vet's, or even ordered their lunch in a café? As adults we have a lot of experience to draw on when it comes to using our imagination. You could say that you have never been to the moon but you could imagine what it might be like to be there. That is because you have amassed lots of information throughout your life that your brain can use for reference. Not many EYFS children have that!

SETTING UP THE SPACE

Equipment: So, you create a space that is full of things that can be anything. It is like that old saying about children getting expensive toys for Christmas and then playing with the box! There is good reason for that: a toy is a toy, but a box has a million possibilities (at least)! Firstly, I have to warn you it doesn't look 'pretty'! It is a pile of boxes, fabric, tubes and crates. The more the children use it the shabbier it will look. But, the level of imagination and language that you will get will be reward enough. The space can change almost by the minute depending on who is playing in it and better than that, you can often have multiple role play scenarios all happening at once based on what the children want to play.

Over time, you can create theme or enhancement boxes which are boxes full of goodies that are linked to a particular child-led interest or theme/topic. When there is an adult leading the play they can use them as a teaching tool. When they leave the play the enhancements are available to the children to either copy the theme of the adult or use in their own non-related play.

Costumes: These are an enhancement for me. I always provide lots of fabric for den making and dressing up and add costumes through the enhancement baskets. When a child has a tabbard with 'police' written across the front they can only role play the police whereas a length of fabric has many, many uses.

Decorating: In terms of 'dressing' or backing the space, I tend just to back it in plain paper and provide cream or black backing paper with lots of mark making tools. The children love creating their own drawings that are personal to their individual play scenarios. I take photos of the children drawing, then photos of them in play using their drawings to play to if a child draws a fire and then role plays being a firefighter and putting it out, they are creating a drawing to play to. Then when the backing sheet is completely full of doodles, you can use it as a display of mark making, adding the photos next to the drawings with a bit of annotation from you about the development of talk/mark making/fine motor skills and so on.

THE ADULT'S ROLE

The role of the adult in moving play forward is sometimes to play alongside children within the context of the role play they have created, and sometimes to offer new language and experience by leading the play. In response to children's interest I would create enhancement boxes that the children could access once they had been introduced into the play. I always have a 'home' box full of the familiar items that you would normally have in your home corner. Then I would create boxes that linked to the theme we were looking at or particular children's interests.

In one nursery class, some children showed a real interest in farms and farming so the teacher enhanced her deconstructed role play space with farm resources. Some were items that she provided and some that the children had asked for, like walkie talkies. She even provided hay which was a very popular move on the part of the children, but a very brave one on the part of the cleaner!

When the adult went into the role play to 'teach' they led the play and set up the boxes and crates to be the farm. They used all of the language and resources to act out (as much as they knew) about being at the farm. When the adult left the role play, the boxes stayed. Some children chose to carry on the farm play. Some took some of the farm resources and used them in their own role play which was nothing to do with the farm, and some didn't use the farm resources at all and played something completely different. All of these scenarios are fine as the 'teaching' session was over and children were interpreting what they had learned in their own way.

Often you will get two or three different role plays happening in the same space at the same time allowing for maximum diversity. This style of role play is perfect for outdoors as well as in.

Small world play

Small world play is a great extension to role play. It supports children's personal, social and emotional development and gives them the opportunity to create their own 'small worlds'. Within these worlds, children can replay and revisit real events that they have encountered in their lives as well as create fantasy worlds from their imaginations, and often a mixture of both. Small world play can be done on an individual level as well as in both small and large groups. It promotes many of the same skills as role play, just acted out through another resource.

Through their play children will have the opportunity to work with others which not only promotes personal and social interaction but also helps to develop communication skills and language. Children will sometimes develop narratives with others, having to listen to and take account of different ideas and negotiate.

Although children will sometimes use small world play to make sense of their own personal world, it can also be a really useful tool to support them in re-enacting a familiar story, sequencing actions and events, and reflecting on experiences and feelings.

Children can develop their problem-solving skills by exploring sets of objects, holding things in their hands and grouping them together, experiencing things that are larger and smaller, using language like 'more' and 'a lot', and counting. Small world play provides mathematical problems to solve: sorting objects by their properties (e.g. putting all the farm animals in the farm), finding out about adding and taking items away from sets, and finding the total number by counting. Children can also explore capacity and size e.g. dressing dolls, building train tracks, and position e.g. putting small world people into a house.

Small world play is also a context for children to expand their understanding of the world, exploring objects with all their senses, finding out about causes and effects (e.g. how pushing the train makes it move along the tracks) and exploring ideas about the world through play (e.g. a garage set, farm or train station). Their physical development is supported with opportunities to develop large and small motor skills and hand-eye co-ordination during play.

Children's creative development is supported as they enjoy and respond to familiar playthings, making noises and movements, and start to pretend and in time to develop stories, sometimes based on their own life experiences. Small world play enables children to be creative and spontaneous in dramatic as well as mundane life situations which interest them. It is often closely related to puppet play and storytelling.

THE IMPORTANCE OF SMALL WORLD PLAY TO CHILDREN'S LEARNING

- It encourages talking (all kinds of language used) and listening (when children play together).

- It allows children to create stories around things they know e.g. people and animals. It also allows children to fantasise about experiences that they have not had themselves.

- It promotes improvisation and the appropriate use of language, including fantasy language.

- It allows children to communicate feelings in a safe way.

- Children can communicate their observations, findings and knowledge about life, books and television.

- It gives children control, allowing them to enter and leave a fictional world at will.

- It encourages children to play together, to self regulate and to exchange ideas.

- It develops an awareness of the feelings and needs of others, as well as the consequences of their actions, leading to natural healthy group relationships.

THE IMPORTANCE OF SMALL WORLD PLAY TO PRACTITIONER'S TEACHING

It enables the adult to discover:

- Children's level of knowledge and understanding.

- Children's ways of thinking.

- Children's attitudes.

- Children's language and communication skills.

- Children's abilities to play in a group.

PROCESSES INVOLVED IN SMALL WORLD PLAY

- Active learning – Using objects and toys such as a dolls' house, a garage, small figures, a floor mat, vehicles, hand puppets, junk materials.

- Imitation – This is not simply copying other children but learning from what they do, and then experimenting with similar roles, behaviour and language.

- Making images – This can be sounds, words or facial expressions all leading to a story or make-believe situation.

- Making symbols – This involves an object representing something else such as a box for a hill or a water tray for a swimming pool. These initially will be highly individual to the child, but gradually the children will use shared symbols agreed by the group.

These processes belong to all forms of representation play, including painting, clay work, domestic play, music and small world toys. They each offer special, unique and worthwhile experiences, allowing the children to express their ideas and feelings, while at the same time developing their relationships with others.

TYPES OF SMALL WORLD PLAY

- Play with animals and other creatures e.g. farm, zoo and domestic animals, prehistoric animals, sea creatures.

- Play with buildings e.g. house, farm, zoo, garage, castle, airport, space station, railway station, bus or fire station, school, shop, hospital, garage.

- Play with a setting e.g. pond, beach, swimming pool, snow scene, swamp, forest, hills, mountains, valleys, space, car park, street, railway line, road layout, field.

- Play with people e.g. all kinds of family figures; a variety of occupations e.g. farmer, soldier, firefighter, space traveller or drivers, fantasy figures e.g. robot, monster, giant.

- Play with vehicles e.g. cars, lorries, trains, rockets, space ships, fire engines, tractors, buses.

- Play with improvised materials/equipment e.g. blocks, bricks, boxes, tins, pebbles, cones, shells, pieces of fabric, carpet, polystyrene, paper.

Children are introduced gradually to each of the above. As their experience and competence improves they should be free to mix and match as well as improvise themselves to create their own imaginary, symbolic scenarios.

Small world play across the EYFS

PERSONAL, SOCIAL AND EMOTIONAL DEVELOPMENT:

- learn how to work independently i.e. selecting small resources for themselves

- learn how to work as part of a group e.g. acting out a drama in the hospital

- learn how to work collaboratively – take turns, share and co-operate

- learn to respect others' ideas

- take care of small world resources – know and understand safety rules

- develop self-expression through manipulating small pieces of equipment in a variety of ways

- become confident at developing ideas using a range of small world resources

- explore feelings, events, worries and concerns using small world resources

- use resources that reflect different cultures

- explore a range of roles with small play people.

PHYSICAL DEVELOPMENT:

- develop fine motor skills and co-ordination through manipulating a range of materials such as play people, farm animals, vehicles

- develop concept of spatial awareness and use space imaginatively e.g. putting furniture into the house, beds in the hospital, cars in the garage

- develop hand/eye co-ordination e.g. threading beads

- use small equipment with confidence, skill and co-ordination.

EXPRESSIVE ARTS AND DESIGN:

- place different types of materials and objects in the small world area for children to create their own furniture, animal enclosures, sheds

- create their own worlds using a range of materials and artefacts.

UNDERSTANDING THE WORLD:

- make links between their play world and their local environment e.g. layout of room in a playhouse and their own house

- develop awareness of the purpose of some features of the local environment e.g. hospital, garage, shops

- talk about people in their local community e.g. farmer, firefighter, pilot, builder, post person, nurse, doctor

- talk about themselves e.g. where they live, their family

- learn about their environment.

MATHEMATICS:

- explore mathematical concepts e.g. pattern, shape, space, size, number, time

- understand and use language related to the above e.g. big, small, wide, light, heavy

- develop mathematical skills e.g. sorting, counting, matching, ordering

- describe the position of people and objects e.g. in, below, above, beside, in front of.

COMMUNICATION AND LANGUAGE:

- talk about their experiences in relation to their model worlds

- talk about their feelings and emotions

- make up their own stories as part of the play

- extend their vocabulary

- develop a range of scenarios for imaginative play

- use books to develop knowledge about different environments e.g. the park, the beach, the zoo

- develop visual discrimination e.g. matching jigsaw pieces to picture.

Using traditional tales

Role playing a story can be a great way for children to confirm and re-visit what they know. But it is even more effective when done as an activity or as an enhancement rather than be the entire theme of your role play. Children love to re-enact familiar tales because they are exactly that, familiar! They have a structure, pattern and often specific language and all of this makes it easy for children to reproduce.

Because they are so familiar and structured it is hard for lots of children to re-interpret them and put their own unique twist on them. I once asked a group of children what else could be under the bridge waiting for the Three Billy Goats Gruff? I was told in no uncertain terms that the answer was 'Nothing!'. When I enquired as to why, the children made it very clear that it had to be a troll because that is what it said in the story! When it comes to a traditional tale, often the story is law!

So traditional tales can be a little bit restrictive for those of your children with a more developed imagination, but they are fantastic for rehearsing children in language, description and story structure. They are also great confidence boosters as you know what is going to happen next, there is no risk in your role playing. You can't make a wrong decision or try and solve a problem without success because the conclusion is already written. When we looked at all of the skills that children could develop through role play earlier in the book, many of them are encapsulated in traditional tale role play, but by no means all. So if you end up in Jack and the Beanstalk's house for a week with some magic beans, a cow mask and several pairs of tights stuffed to the gusset, painted green and strung up to the ceiling … your play might be just a little bit stifled!

GOLDILOCKS AND THE THREE BEARS

As a student I went to observe a reception teacher who had spent a long time creating a role play area based around the Goldilocks story. She had covered her wooden play frame in brick printed paper, there was a window with a café curtain, a red gingham tablecloth with three bowls on it (large, medium sized and small), three spoons, three chairs … strangely no beds. Even though these are integral to the story, she couldn't fit them in so she missed them out. To be fair it would be quite hard to get three beds into the average role play area!

When the children saw it, they loved it (for about a day). They had read the big book version of the story several times and now it was time to go and play. The problem is, it turned out that there is not a huge amount you can do in the Three Bears house other than make porridge and argue over who is going to be Goldilocks! One little boy decided that he wasn't going to be Mummy Bear or Goldilocks because they were both girls so he decided to be Daddy Bear. A great part for a boisterous boy! The big book that they had

been reading had really reinforced the fact that Daddy Bear was very cross with Goldilocks and 'in his big, gruff voice he would say' Who's been…' and so on. So our 'Daddy Bear' digs down deep to find his inner gruffness and off he goes, loudly! 'Who has been sitting in MY chair'. At which point the slightly less gruff, but never the less loud voice of the adult sailed across the ether with the immortal phrase 'That's an outside voice! Keep it down or you will have to come out!'. Well, if you can't be Daddy Bear and you don't want to be a 'girl's part' then you have only really got Baby Bear left.

Of course there is a fatal flaw in that assumption, because like father like son, Baby Bear is a bit of a shouter, or should that be wailer? Before too long we were being treated to a dramatic interpretation of Baby Bear's lamentations 'Someone's been sitting in my chair, eating my porridge etc'. Unfortunately the budding Olivier didn't get much further than the chair before he was instructed to leave the role play as a result of being told about his loud voice for the 'second' time! I can't imagine he was desperate to get back in there any time soon!

If the children are showing a real interest in a story that you are reading then try and create separate role play space where they can play and explore the familiar. If you haven't got that much space then create a resource basket linked to the familiar tale and let the children who want to play within that theme enhance the space using the resources. Then when their play is over, the space can become something completely different.

Like Goldilocks really, you want your traditional tales role play to be not too directed and not too open-ended – you need it just right!

Outdoor role play

I have had lots of success working with settings on deconstructed role play indoors. But I really wanted to look closely at the role play of children role playing outside. By the very nature that it is outdoor, it tends to be less 'themed' and linked to topic, so there is more scope for individual exploration and development.

I was working with one particular setting on a den-making project. Partly the project was centred around what children could achieve in continuous provision outdoors, both in their capabilities to build exciting and complex structures and also the opportunities for role play development that something as open-ended as a den could give them.

The setting I was working with was a three-form entry where the primary and reception classes share a large outdoor space (also shared by an on-site but independent day nursery). During the project, although they don't have 'playtime' (the three reception classes don't go out together), they have an allotted time slot in the morning and afternoon where they go out as a class. (By the end of the project this was running as continuous outdoor provision!) I spent my first morning observing the role play of the children from each class in turn. In terms of role play opportunities that had been created by the adults they had two choices. Each was placed at opposite ends of the outdoor space.

Themed role play: the pirate ship

I am not the world's biggest fan of this type of outdoor structure. Although it has some pluses I have always found that boats, trains and so on can really limit children's imagination because they can only ever really be one thing. That is why when I work with settings on establishing an outdoor area I encourage them to keep their structures as non-descript and multifunctional as possible. Throughout your entire early years environment, indoors and out, you want to ensure a significant level of ambiguity. Ambiguous resources can really encourage children to use their imaginations and also free them from the constraints of definite objects only being used for their original purpose where a sheep is a sheep and a till is a till!

Deconstructed role play: den making

This is a quick to assemble space full of things that can be anything along with a selection of 'real' objects selected by the children to enhance their play at any one particular time.

Both this and the pirate ship have their uses, but in my opinion, the ship is far more limited. What it is good for is giving a first-hand experience of something that has got all of the main features of a real ship. If you couldn't visit an actual ship this would be a lot better than a cardboard box. But it will always be a ship and as for the cardboard box, well ... it can be a million things, but only if the child has had experience of a million things to transpose onto the box.

Deconstructed role play does not work as well if it is just a pile of boxes. It is important to enhance the boxes with 'real' objects for children who need that first-hand experience. If I am working with a setting to introduce this sort of role play, I have found that it is best not to just clear away the 'vet's' and dump a load of boxes. There needs to be a period of introduction and modelling for the children so I usually take away most of the structure and ask the children what they would like the area to be and then work with them to build it, theme it and enhance it. As they get more used to the process, they will do this independently which allows for greater freedom of play.

Children can only effectively use deconstructed role play if they have a prior knowledge of real events and real objects that they can transfer to the boxes and other materials using their imaginations. The more limited their experience, the more limited their play.

What I found on my initial visit is that even though a nice collection of den-making resources had been provided, not many children engaged with them independently and those that did soon gave up. A significant number went to play on the pirate ship and stayed playing there for a considerable amount of time. What it is very easy to do on occasions like this is to look at the engagement of the children on the pirate ship and then make the assumption that they are learning, when in fact it is often the case that you will come across high level engagement but low level play/attainment.

My next step with the pirate ship play was to observe and record which skills the children were encountering, employing and rehearsing both in terms of language and social interaction. What I found was that their play remained very 'static'. The children who were playing in the space tended to take on very tried, tested and familiar 'pirate' roles. As their knowledge of the intricacies of the pirate world was limited, they tended to repeat the same 'good guy, bad guy' scenario, mainly based on a version of Peter Pan.

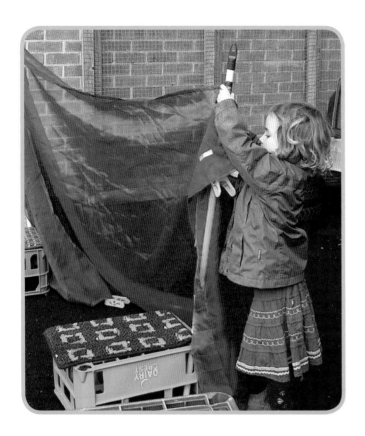

Each time I visited to observe, the play was always very similar. Children took on familiar roles which played themselves out in a predictable way towards the same conclusion. While I acknowledge that for some children at the early stages of their development this familiar play is supportive and consolidating, for the children I was observing this play was low level and lacking in challenge. Rather than take away their access to the pirate ship or try to upskill them in their knowledge of all things pirate, my plan was to use den-making as a possible alternative.

What I have found with den-making projects is, if you give children a pile of den-making equipment they will have a go but they often get frustrated at the fact that their dens won't stay up or take too long to build. What they need are a few simple demonstrations and key ideas – then they are off! Usually I build a den for the children, then take it straight down. I then build one with the children and take it down again, then get them to build it a third time with little or no support. It is the infinite possibilities that are great with den-making outdoors. Even if it all falls down, it doesn't matter because you can rebuild it. Much the same as a deconstructed role play space indoors: a den-making space outdoors is individual to children who are using it at the time.

Outdoor domestic role play: mud kitchen

Domestic play runs through the very core of children's role play. It is the play that is most familiar to them and the play they return to most. It doesn't always take place in a 'house'. You will see children translate their domestic play through fish in the water tray, lumps of dough on the malleable materials table and toys in the small world. As it is so pivotal to children's learning it is important that we support it both indoors and out. What better way to support domestic play outdoors than with a mud kitchen?

A mud kitchen is not the same as a soil or digging pit, although they are a good place to start. A mud kitchen will have some structure and be a defined space, that is well resourced that children can return to again and again. You do not need to spend a fortune when you are creating a mud kitchen. Unless you want to put it away every night (trust me, if they are well used you won't!) then you need some structures that you can leave outside all year round. You can go from purpose built outdoor spaces to DIY crates, tables and old shelving units that you can beg, steal or borrow. It is worth remembering, that any wooden indoor furniture you use will eventually warp due to the sun and rain. If you can, varnish anything you leave out with a good yacht varnish to help to protect it. Although shelving is important for storage, ample work surface is really important. You need to provide enough working space, at child height, to allow the children to arrange all of the resources that they need and then carry out their stirring, mixing, pouring and creating. All of which takes up a great deal of space!

As with any play space, the size of your kitchen will help to determine the type of play that takes place in it. A larger, freer space will encourage larger, often more physical, play. A smaller more intimate space will encourage smaller scale play involving less children. Of course you can only work with the space that you have got, but if you can provide an area where several children can work together that is sub-divided into larger and smaller spaces, that would be ideal. If you only have a small space for your mud kitchen then put it next to other areas that have strong links to that sort of play like den making, or large block play. The spaces can then run as separate entities in their own right or link depending on the preferences of the children.

When it comes to creating and resourcing your mud kitchen, the first thing to do is to ask the children what they would like: they will always have some definite ideas. Be prepared for your mud kitchen to 'evolve' as the children play in it because although the structure is likely to stay the same, how the children play with the resources will be different. The children are going to be exploring and consolidating a range of skills like: filling, pouring, emptying, transferring, mixing, gathering, decanting, stirring, whisking, scooping, ladling, grinding, handling, moulding, patting, smoothing, mark making, throwing, splatting, splashing, sharing out, serving, foraging, selecting, picking, collecting, garnishing, shredding, frothing, crushing, mashing, measuring, adding, brewing, sieving, filtering and separating to name but a few. So it is worth considering how you will resource your space to support these skills.

Young children like to work and be in small spaces that make them feel secure, but also private. Mud kitchens benefit from fences and walls as not only do they give the children the sense of enclosure, they are also great for hanging things from. Of course, ideally you need to be able to see your children at play, both for the purposes of observation and health and safety. Your walls therefore do not have to be full height, you can create half height structures using mesh or fencing. Your mud kitchen still needs to feel like part of the outdoor space so that children will use it as part of the natural flow of their play and not see it as somewhere that they have to go to as a completely separate entity. If it is easy to access, then the children will use it.

Even though we call it a mud kitchen, it is not just about mud. Mud is a great starting point so ideally you need to set up your mud kitchen near to a good source of soil. If you haven't got an open digging space that the children can access, then you can provide low level containers of top soil that the children can use to make their mud mixes. Sand is also a good addition to a mud kitchen. Basically, anything that will help the children to experience different consistencies, colours and textures while they are mixing.

Of course, to make soil into mud you need water! If you can have a running water supply or sink in your mud kitchen that is great, but if not different sized containers and buckets are ideal for children to engage in transporting their own water supply. For lots of children, this fetching and carrying of the water is very much part of the play so a water source that is not directly linked to your kitchen is not such a bad thing. Washing-up liquid, scented shampoo, powder paint and even a bit of glitter can all make simple but effective additions to your mud kitchen mixes. Children will get the opportunity to experiment and create to their hearts' content. If you can, try and provide a wide selection of different natural resources for children to add to their play such as pebbles, gravel, bark, wood chips, seeds, pine cones – the list is never ending!

Children will also want to pick leaves and flowers to add to their mud mixes. If you are going to set up a kitchen, then you need to have a conversation with the children about what they are allowed to pick and what they aren't. It is very hard to make petal perfume without petals. By the same token, every flower in your setting could easily be stripped of its petals in one afternoon by a group of over-zealous perfume makers! You need to establish a middle ground.

THE ADULT'S ROLE

It is important that all members of your team not only appreciate the domestic play that children will develop through the mud kitchen, but the potential for learning that exists in manipulating mud. The role of the adult then is to support children in their play, facilitating learning by offering up ideas and also by encouraging children to make their own discoveries through the use of open questioning and the posing of problems to be solved. It is important that we think beyond the domesticity and help children to investigate and make connections to their understanding of the world.

HEALTH AND SAFETY!

Dogs, cats and foxes all like a nicely dug soil patch to use as a toilet, so you have to be vigillant to ensure that the children aren't going to come into contact with any animal poo as it can be extremely harmful. If you want to be absolutely safe then you can buy the soil for your mud kitchen from the garden centre, rather than dig it up from your outdoor area. If you are going to buy it then you need to use loam top soil and not compost. Compost, although an interesting addition to your mud kitchen, does not behave in the same way as soil, therefore you don't get the same sort of result in your mixing!

Hand washing is essential after any mud play. Because you are not going to be with the children every time they finish their mud kitchen play, it is really important that the hand washing routine becomes automatic to them. It is also good to get the children to wash up all of the utensils they have used in the kitchen using warm soapy water. Not only do they enjoy the water play, but it also really helps to keep their hands clean. A little squirt of sanitiser never goes amiss either!

Superhero and weapon play

When I first trained to teach in the early years, gun play was definitely off limits. We were told that there should be a zero tolerance as it encouraged children to be rough and aggressive. Any sign of a child wielding anything that might have even been slightly mistaken for a gun had to be dealt with quickly and sternly. I remember being left with the feeling that if I ignored this behavior then I would be turning all of my gun-making children into thugs in later life.

It occurred to me after a few years, that no matter what sort of cohort the children were, no matter which school I was teaching in, superhero and weapon play was a big part of significant number of children's play of choice. I seemed to spend an inordinate of time saying 'I hope that is not a gun' about something that clearly was. The only positive to that was it encouraged children to think quickly and be creative in their responses like 'No, erm, it's a, erm, it's a hose! I am watering the plants!'. An admittedly unusual action in a game of chase! Not only was I seeing how much enjoyment children got out of it but also how much potential teaching and learning I was missing from their high level engagement. It also seemed like such a natural and fundamental play response for so many children that I figured there had to be more to it.

Establish a policy

So, around the time that I became a headteacher and needed to have a definite policy on how this sort of play would be judged in our school, I began to look into it in more depth. Through what I found out and the subsequent practice and impact that I have observed since, I have completely changed my view. Now I wouldn't have a setting without a good dollop of superhero and weapon play in it. But, and there always is a but, practitioners need to understand why children naturally play that way and how they can support and expend that play without instigating World War III!

One of the reasons that children play in that way is that it gives them an opportunity to explore their interpretations of what they see going on in the world around them. By that I don't just mean in the playground and at home but also in the media. How many children's films, even by Disney, contain large sections of physical combat and power struggles? Increasingly when I am engaged in talk sessions with groups of children, they will tell me about films they have watched with older siblings or parents, computer games that they have played or news reports that they have watched, all of which contain graphic images and often quite extreme violence. Even if they haven't actually seen it for themselves, lots of children will relive a 'version' of what took place in the retelling of the child that did. No matter how cautious and careful we are as parents, our children cannot escape the reality of the world around them – especially when their influencers become not just their parents and carers but also their peers!

MAKING SENSE OF THE WORLD

Because children don't have the same vast catalogue of experience that most adults have, when they experience the world around them then they have to try and make some sense of it. Before it makes any sense, they have to get what they think they experienced clear in their heads. The way to do this is to re-visit and re-live it and the easiest way to do that is through role play.

Role play allows children to explore all of these questions and emotions in a controlled environment and a safe context. They can explore what is possible and, equally as importantly, what is impossible. Exploring what is risky and dangerous through play is essential if we want our children to be able to acknowledge and accept the limits of reality. There is a huge element of emotional exploration that goes on during this sort of play. Through power struggle and combat, children can put themselves into semi-real situations that allow them to experience and combat negative emotions.

In a nursery I was working in recently, a child ran into the role play area and told all of the children that a crocodile was coming to eat them up. Panic ensued, with children demonstrating some real emotion through play. All was made right in the end by the boy who had alerted us all to crocodile and he turned out to be Batman in disguise (phew!) and he killed the crocodile. For him there was a real sense of being in a position of power and achievement. He was allowed to feel strong and in control. For him it was not about the violent act of killing the crocodile, it was about how the play scenario enabled him to feel.

INTERPRETING THEIR PLAY

As adults, we tend to be far more literal in our interpretations of children's superhero and weapon play, so when we see play fighting we see violence and aggression as the main catalysts for the play, which is rarely the case. I am not saying that play fighting doesn't sometimes turn into actual aggression, but that this was not the intention when the play started out. If it was, then it wouldn't be play, it would just be a fight!

By its very nature this sort of play involves struggle, chase, competition and noise! It is often adrenalin-fuelled play, and because there is a high level of thrill for the children taking part it will be fast and loud. We cannot penalise children for that. If we accept that this sort of play is going to take place then we need to make provision for it, both inside and out, and make sure that the whole team have clear expectations about what is acceptable and what isn't. In cultures where they do not have guns, it is interesting to note that children still engage in this type of play, only their guns are replaced with spears, bows and arrows. It is the same symbolism. Speaking of symbolism, is there any difference between children playing 'robbers' and pointing guns at each other and children playing Harry Potter and pointing their wands to cast spells and kill each other? Does it feel better because it is not a gun? Surely the end result is the same thing? It is just that the symbolism is more acceptable to adults. Whether we like it or not, for the vast majority of us, guns are part of our everyday life and culture. Our children are surrounded by them in the images that they see and the television that they watch. Even programmes aimed specifically at children contain characters with guns, or their symbolic equivalent.

The question that we have to ask ourselves is: when our children are engaged in gun play, are they practising to become an adult with a gun or are they just exploring emotions such as control, risk and a sense of power. Lots of our children's essential emotional connections, consolidation and development can be made through fantasy play. The more opportunity they get to rehearse them, the more proficient they will get at managing them.

Children have always had an appetite for the macabre. They like a 'scare' but they also like the fact that in a play situation, it can always be alright in the end. You only have to look at the universal success of fairy stories with children across the world and across the ages. They exist in every culture and often follow a surprisingly similar pattern. There is always a good helping of pain and misery, but justice is served in the end. The practice of destroying your world and then putting it back together again is an important process for children to enable them to separate fantasy and reality. Our children are ultimately powerless until they acquire a significant level of independence, which doesn't usually come for them until well into their childhood (even if then). Through superhero and weapon type role play children can learn to manage their own feelings by displacing them. They can make things turn out as they want them to, reinvent the truth and explore other possible outcomes that wouldn't be possible in 'real' life where there is only one.

Wrestling, chasing and play fighting all help children to experience 'safe' danger, assess risk and take appropriate action. As a species we are 'hunter gatherers' and much of the way that children play is grounded in instinct and an innate desire to hone our survival skills. Our experience of current culture just dressed them differently from our days in the cave! Through this type of play children get to see a direct correlation between cause and effect. In any activity that involves an element of speed or physical interaction there is a likelihood that someone might experience a bump here and there. How their reactions directly affect the physical and emotional well-being of others is a crucial life lesson. If you don't get the chance to experience it through play then you will have to learn when it is happening for real, and that can have far more devastating consequences for everyone concerned.

MANAGING AGGRESSIVE PLAY

If children's weapon play does spill over into actual aggressive fighting then this needs to be investigated as a separate issue. It is not the play that is the problem, but why the player chose to take their actions in that particular direction. Most often, but not always, these children are boys who are attracted helplessly to this play for five key reasons:

- making guns is an achievable task

- weapon play relates to early communications skills

- major themes of children's play are represented in weapon-related playing

- running in big spaces or outside is a preferred play style

- it is a universal language.

It is not that girls don't have the desire to experience and experiment feelings of power and control, but they tend to express their feelings more through language and relationships than they do through physical play. There has been significant research and discussion about why this might be. The root most probably lies in the social stereotyping that boys and girls experience from birth. Girls are encouraged not to be as aggressive in their physical behaviour and to take on a 'different' role which is socially acceptable for their gender. But, you cannot eradicate the need to explore innate emotion and use of language is the next best thing. When I reflect on my own experience in the classroom, it is true that I certainly had more issues around relationships and 'she said this ...' than I did with the boys.

There are lots of important strategies that children have to use when they are engaged in this play: they have to become rule makers, organisers and negotiators to name but a few. If they do not develop these skills effectively then the play breaks down quickly and they lose the opportunity to play in a way that they really enjoy. Superhero play provides positive symbols of power that children can take on. For the vast majority of them their day-to-day life offers no other experience like this.

The truth is, almost anything can be a gun: a pointed finger, construction, sticks and balloons are easily used as guns, swords, light sabers, magic wands. Weapons are on the whole very easy to create. What children soon realise is that with their creation of a weapon comes an immediate sense of power which is primarily because of the association that adults and other children have with weapon play. If you point your gun at me and say 'bang' I might drop down dead (you have all of the power), I might run away (you have all of the power), I might say 'I hope that isn't a gun?!' (you still have the power because you solicited that response from me). Not only are you amassing a catalogue of possible emotional responses to your actions, you are also learning a great deal about communication and how you can communicate your thoughts and feelings to others in a variety of ways, some with more success than others, but all valid nevertheless.

POWER GAMES

Children's play, although dressed differently, often revolves around the same central themes, because it is these themes that children are most familiar with and that dominate their everyday life; issues like death, loneliness, being lost or alone and illness. Superhero and weapon play certainly provides opportunities for these themes to be explored and all of these themes have a similar dominant element that I have talked about before, namely power, and being in control or controlled by others. Children are quick to identify the people who have the power roles in their lives, their parents, teachers, carers. It is these characters that children will most mimic in their role play, acting out familiar interactions.

In order to make sense of these relationships in their play, children often test out their own ideas. Children have lots of questions about the world around them, many of which they cannot articulate because they are too subtly attached to emotion. It is these questions that they explore through their role play. It is a given that children will play at what concerns and worries them. They play at what causes them anxiety. Usually the place of choice to act out your superhero or gun play fantasy is outside. As I have said previously this sort of play usually involves chase and noise, so outside is the perfect place to do it where your movements can be bigger and your voices louder. In addition to the social and emotional benefits, children also have the opportunity to develop and consolidate their gross motor development, balance, hand-eye co-ordination and critical thinking.

I have observed many sessions of this sort of play in settings where there have been a mixture of children with a mixture of languages, very few of whom spoke English. So much of this type of play relies on non verbal cues — it has a universal language all of its own. The rules are very simple: you are 'a goody' or 'a baddy', 'the chased' or 'the chaser'. You know when you have been 'got' and you know when you have 'got away'. What could be simpler? It can be difficult for settings to know where to start when it comes to managing superhero and weapon play. When not proactively managed it can appear to get out of hand very quickly, become too aggressive and too loud and that is when the play is often closed down.

MANAGING THE PLAY

There are two key things that really help in the management of this type of play. The first is to give it value. It will never work if you just walk in and say 'right, from tomorrow we are promoting gun play!' All of the adults involved have to be really clear about why you are supporting weapon play as a setting and the many benefits that can be gained from it. I often find in my work with settings that once adults are more confident in what it is that they are actually looking at, they are far more able to facilitate that play effectively.

The second is to create a policy before you start. It is often through the discussions that come about when you are creating a collective policy that you can iron out misconceptions and explore possible anxieties. If your whole team is not on board then it is likely that the initiative will be less successful and could ultimately fail. I have included an example of a policy as an Appendix to the book. It is by no means the 'definitive' superhero and weapon play 'policy', but it will certainly get you started.

When superhero and weapon play is not permitted, children lose out on developing key skills as a player. They also pick up very negative messages around education and how their own preferences, needs and desires fit in with our education agenda as adults. These negative messages are likely to affect their engagement in learning full stop. Children who have their starting points for play blocked at an early age may not achieve their potential because they do not feel positive about themselves as learners. I often (too often) find myself saying 'High level attainment comes from high level engagement'. If we disengage our learners then we are significantly jeopardising their potential for their attainment.

Often weapon play is referred to as being low quality or 'empty' play, as it just seems to involve aggressive interactions. Tina Bruce published 12 indicators of quality play (see opposite). If you match these to the sort of experiences that children have during weapon play you can see that it is anything but low quality or empty. It has the potential to be the complete opposite.

The 12 indicators of play

The following indicators are adapted from two books on play published by Tina Bruce (1991, 1996):

1 Using first-hand experiences

2 Making up rules

3 Making props

4 Choosing to play

5 Rehearsing the future

6 Pretending

7 Playing alone

8 Playing together

9 Having a personal agenda

10 Being deeply involved

11 Trying out recent learning

12 Co-ordinating ideas, feelings and relationships for free-flow play.

WEAPON PLAY CASE STUDY

Initially I was invited to work with a setting to look at how we could utilise their outdoor space in a more productive way, especially in relation to communication and mark-making. The space, although large, had been decked within an inch of its life and the entire space had been 'zoned' into very prescribed spaces. Far from encouraging the children to explore and create, it very much limited their play to the very prescriptive type of space and equipment that had been installed (at great cost).

After an evaluation of the usage of the outdoor space, our plan was to create a den-making area. The equipment that was in the area we chose was already fixed permanently, and although not great for the development needs of the children, it provided some good anchors for washing lines and other den-making paraphernalia!

But as with the best strategies it didn't go exactly according to plan … we ended up having a slight change of plan for the den-making area outdoors. It came up as a result of a discussion about the 'boy's' play! Basically: any object becomes a gun and they chase. There is lots of imagination going on but they literally run through everything – so lots of work is being (unintentionally) interrupted or destroyed. In my book it is perfectly acceptable to say to the boys that they can play their game but not when it destroys the work of other children because that is inappropriate. It was suggested that we 'ban' gun play – but I know from experience that that would be fruitless as they we would just drive it underground and they would do it anyway.

So … I asked the team to identify the play that the boys were engaging in. I also asked them to accept that it was 'normal' play for children of this age and talked a bit about why they play that way. I then asked the team how we could use that play to our advantage rather than fight against it. If the boys only ever run around day after day playing the same game in an environment as big as ours you have to ask what is not going on in the other areas to tempt them. The upshot is that we decided to turn the soon to be den-making area into an army camp where they can act out their gun play but we can intervene and use it as a teaching opportunity.

We also talked about having a target shooting area to encourage/assess number recognition/bonds! Obviously not real shooting but an activity based around that theme. When this was mentioned the staff all said how much the children (particularly, but not exclusively, boys) would love that and how the engagement levels would be really high.

Which brings me back to my well worn point … If you know that they do it and will do it even if you tell them not to, then do your job and use it as an opportunity to educate – both about the reality of guns and to teach them something.

 In play a child always behaves beyond his average age, above his daily behavior. In play it is as though he were a head taller than himself.
Lev Vygotsky

Setting up a 'Boot Camp'

1 Why? You need to identify the reason for setting it up.

'Outdoor observations have shown that there is an ongoing trend for very physical active play, that is mainly initiated and dominated by boys, that involves gun, superhero or combative play. Although not malicious, this play is disrupting and in some cases destroying other focused work that is taking place outdoors. The 'management' of this play is not only taking up valuable practitioner time but also stifling the opportunities that the play itself presents. Of all of the types and themes of play that we have identified outside this half term, this is the only one that has been consistently observed on a daily basis.'

2 Specific needs identified – what exactly is it that you need to tackle?

'The play that we have identified mainly consists of groups of boys who have an ongoing game in which they chase each other with the purpose of capture or shooting. At the moment they are using any non-specific item to represent a weapon and occasionally creating one from construction. One of the issues that we have identified is that the children are using inappropriate items in their play which result in either damage to the item or loss. This in turn has an impact on the overall level of provision that we can offer when resources are damaged or incomplete. Even though practitioners remind these children regularly about how to play, they become very highly engaged in their play and 'forget'. This high level of engagement, from a group of children who are often more difficult to engage, needs to be utilised not ignored.'

3 What other elements of their play can you use to help?

'Our observation has also shown us that these children show high levels of engagement in the deconstructed outdoor role play, especially the building of den-like structures with the community play blocks and tarpaulins.'

4 Which elements of the curriculum will you be supporting through this provision?

Personal, social and emotional development

The children will be working together developing skills of sharing, complying and negotiating. They will have the opportunity to plan, discuss, build and amend their plans. The den play will allow children to produce spaces where they can feel secure and enclosed. The gun/superhero play will give them the opportunity to assimilate what they see around them and make some sense of it within their own personal context.

Communication and language

We will provide lots of opportunities for mark-making, drawing and planning. The level of engagement will allow us to introduce a great deal of language development and vocabulary. This will need just the right amount of practitioner intervention, which we will review regularly. We will enhance the area with related books as appropriate.

Physical development

The large scale construction will develop children's spatial awareness as well as their sense of balance and proportion. The process will involve both gross and fine motor movement which will impact on the children's dexterity and impact upon their mark-making ability.

Understanding the world

Through the construction process the children will be getting first-hand experience how and why things work, the effects of the weather on the structures that they build and which materials are most appropriate. The opportunities for knowledge in this area are limitless. Again there needs to be careful and considered adult intervention which is regularly reviewed.

Mathematics

The children will have the opportunity to develop their understanding and use of mathematical language especially related to size, length and weight.

Expressive arts and design

Children will be encouraged to develop their higher order thinking skills, finding solutions to problems and coming up with ideas for building their structures. They will then use those structures to support their imaginative play.

5 Any specific interventions to encourage maximum engagement from the children?

'We are aware that this is a 'boy' dominated area of our outdoor provision at the moment. As such we need to make sure that we use specific planned interventions to try and make this area more engaging to the girls. Our observations have shown us so far that the boys tend to do the 'construction' and the girls then do the enhancement of the structure and often lead the play. The boys are very self-sufficient in their play and will often initiate an activity. The girls tend to engage better when there is also an adult present. It appears that if the girls do initiate den construction and are then joined by a group of boys then the boys dominate and take over. Our adult intervention in the play needs to take all of the above into account and actively combat any negative aspects.'

6 What will you create? Using what you know.

'Our initial plan is to create a designated area that responds to the preferred play and personal interests of a significant number of our children. Rather than attempt to 'ban' or ignore play that is causing us issues but results in high levels of engagement, we are going to utilise it to achieve maximum learning impact. We will establish a den-making area based around an 'army/combat' theme. The children will lead the content through a collaborative planning session. We will provide some commercial representations of weapons as well as work with the children on how to produce their own.

We will establish rules about how this area is to be used and what is acceptable when it comes to weapon play. We will also be clear about the sanctions that we will put in place if the play becomes inappropriate. Because we have identified that the engagement of girls in this type of play can often be an issue, we will ensure that they are involved in the planning process and implement as many of their ideas as possible. To ensure specific impact on learning we will look at the current needs of the children, identified by our most recent assessment, and see which of these identified needs could be met through planning activities based on this area.

We will continually carry out observations of how the area is working and evaluate its success at team meetings.

So how did it work out?

Half a term later we evaluated our progress.

'Meanwhile at 'Boot Camp' things are progressing really well. We have almost eradicated the anti-social, disruptive play in the outdoor area. Because it is now confined to one space the children are investing far more time and energy in creating 'game play' rather than just chasing. There is negotiation and discussion as well as some arguments over who gets the best guns! My feeling on that is that children will never learn how to resolve an argument if they are not allowed to have one!

We were experiencing children hitting each other with the swords even though we had made clear our policy on no body contact. To combat this trend, one of our staff gave the children fencing lessons stressing that the more skill you had the less body contact there would be. It worked a treat – we will just have to see if they remember. What is important with an area like this is that you set ground rules and stick to them. No second chances: if you break the rule you are out – end of!'

Superhero and weapon play policy

This is an example of a superhero and weapon play policy that was created and amended over a period of time, whilst working with a number of settings who were looking at supporting this kind of play. It is by no means a definitive policy, but it has got all of the essential bits in it to get you talking and thinking. I would strongly recommend that you don't just insert your setting or school name into the banks and stick it in your policy folder! For an initiative like this to be really successful, ALL staff, senior leadership, governors and parents have to be aware of what you are going to do and why it is so beneficial.

A full downloadable copy of this policy that you can copy and paste can be found in the resources section of my blog: www.abcdoes.com.

CONTENTS

◆ Introduction

◆ Rationale

◆ Aims

◆ Equal opportunities and inclusion

◆ Principles that underpin the policy

◆ Initial preparations

◆ Creating an appropriate environment

◆ Building on what children know and understand

◆ Partnership with parents

◆ Continuing Professional Development (CPD)

◆ Appendices

Introduction

Most children enjoy engaging in imaginative play that relates to, and makes sense of, the world that they live in. For lots of children (particularly boys) this imaginative play contains a strong element of weapon and superhero re-enactment. Re-enacting weapon use is a universal language of play for children and usually results in high levels of engagement for the children actively involved in it.

Images and ideas gleaned from the media are common starting points in boys' play and may involve characters with special powers or weapons. Adults can find this type of play particularly challenging and have a natural instinct to stop it. This is not necessary as long as practitioners help the boys to understand and respect the rights of other children and to take responsibility for the resources and environment. As the EYFS states:

Value play which is based on people, such as superheroes who may mean a lot to children, even if you do not appreciate them yourself!

(EYFS Principles into Practice card 4.1 Learning and Development)

(DCSF 2007)

Creating situations so that boys' interests in these forms of play can be fostered through healthy and safe risk-taking will enhance every aspect of their learning and development.

A child loves his play, not because it's easy, but because it's hard.

Benjamin Spock

Rationale

At

_____

we feel it is important to create a whole-school approach of which staff, children, parents, governors and other agencies have a clear understanding. This policy is a formal statement of our approach to children's weapon and superhero imaginative play.

Aims

The commitments linked to the principle of Learning and Development help us to understand how children learn actively through play, first-hand experiences, creativity and critical thinking. As children learn and develop, they 'actively build their own meanings by applying, revising and reapplying what they know'. (EYFS, Effective Practice relating to card 4.2 Active Learning). Boys often appear to be more active learners than girls, but whether or not there is a gender divide in this respect, active learners need opportunities to make their own decisions and have control over their learning to keep their interest and to develop their creativity.

Equal Opportunities and Inclusion

The children and parents are actively involved in the education process at

_____

and their perceptions about weapon and superhero play are explored and valued.

The staff will regularly evaluate the impact that actively fostering this element of role play has on the environment, the cohort as a whole and identified groups of children and individuals.

If required a range of support strategies will be put in place to ensure that this style of play does not have any negative impact.

Principles that underpin the policy

The principles that underpin our transition policy are:

★ Approaches to teaching and learning in role play should reflect the interests of the children and not exclusively those of the adults.

★ Planning for role play in the environment should be based upon assessment information from the observed play of the current cohort.

★ Our setting will acknowledge the positive aspects of the character of the superhero and highlight the negative aspects of weapon use and physical violence at a level that is appropriate to the age and needs of the children. This will be mainly done through story, drama and appropriate discussion.

★ Styles of teaching and learning should meet the needs of children and not pre-conceived notions of what is or is not appropriate role play.

★ All children's emotional welfare, well-being and involvement should be assessed in relation to this style of play.

★ Children should enjoy the play opportunity.

★ The weapon/superhero play should motivate and challenge children.

★ The creation of an effective culture of weapon/superhero play in any setting takes time, and is a process rather than an event.

★ Parents and carers need to feel well informed about and comfortable with the settings approach to weapon/superhero play and the principals that underpin it.

★ Children, parents/carers and staff need to be involved on an equal basis in the formulation and regular review of this policy.

★ Effective and engaging play is about our setting fitting the interests of the child, not the child fitting the setting.

★ Ongoing opportunities for quality imaginative play are not overlooked or left to chance, but thought about and planned in advance.

Initial preparations

All staff across our setting must be aware of the thinking that underpins this policy and build its review into our self-evaluation schedule.

▨ All staff to observe children's individual and group imaginative play within the setting identifying themes that result in high level engagement.

▨ Time allocated within planning meetings to discuss the ongoing development and management of the settings approach to weapon/superhero play.

▨ Case studies, further reading and research into this type of play is made available for parent, carer and practitioner reference within the setting.

▨ An appropriate space both indoor and outdoor is designated for the development of this style of play.

▨ Resources and enhancements (including appropriate construction materials) are put in place to specifically support this style of play.

▨ Arrangements are made for passing on information to parents about how/why the setting will use, manage and enhance weapon/superhero play.

▨ This policy will be shared with all staff and managing/governing bodies as its content will impact on other adults' approaches to weapon/superhero play in other areas of the setting.

Creating an appropriate environment

The types of play that boys and girls engage in is enhanced or diminished by the quality of the learning environment inside and out. The EYFS card, The Environment for Learning, flags up that: 'Children need sensitive, knowledgeable adults who know when and how to engage their interests and how to offer support at different times.' (card 3.2) Practitioners must take responsibility for ensuring the learning environment is planned to inspire, challenge and intrigue every child. However, sometimes practitioners find the chosen play of boys more difficult to understand and value than that of girls. They may choose activities in which adults involve themselves least, or play that involves more action and a greater use of the available space, especially outdoors.

> Some boys who are at risk of becoming disaffected at a very young age have shown significant improvements if their learning takes place outside. Opportunities which reflect all six areas of learning outdoors must be available.
>
> **(Bilton et al 2005.)**

Practitioners need to be aware of the impact of both the emotional and physical environment on the well-being and self-esteem of all children.

Practitioners will:

→ involve themselves as much in the boys' choices of role play and learning experiences as the girls'

→ see the physical environment as one of the most powerful resources through which children can learn, and carefully plan and monitor how it is used

→ value the outdoor as much as the indoor environment, thinking creatively about the environment and how it can support weapon/superhero role play

→ experiences and activities we have on offer ensure we meet the needs of boys as well as girls

→ are aware that sometimes an interest may be sparked by something immediate in the environment, or something much more long term, such as interest in weapon/superhero play

→ ensure role play areas incorporate boys' play themes allowing children to fetch and move resources from one place to another, to enhance their play themes

→ ensure all children take equal responsibility in caring for the environment of the setting, tidying up and looking after equipment and each other, fostering a sense of social responsibility.

> Play energizes us and enlivens us. It eases our burdens. It renews our natural sense of optimism and opens us up to new possibilities.
>
> **Stuart Brown, MD**

> A child who does not play is not a child, but the man who does not play has lost forever the child who lived in him.
>
> **Pablo Neruda**

Building on what children know and understand

will ensure that, through training and development, all staff are aware of the impact of both the emotional and physical environment on the well-being and self-esteem of all children.

We will:

● ensure that there are regular opportunities for 'unplanned' role play to allow for children's self-expression and staff observation

● monitor, record and evaluate the positive aspects of the play that they see, incorporating preferences and themes into future planning

● ensure that the physical environment both indoor and outdoor contains resources that will support and promote children's play

● provide a variety of resources , some that replicate actual objects alongside others that will be open-ended and ambiguous to allow for individual interpretation and foster an approach of imagination and creativity

● be aware that the success of some themes and enhancements will differ between cohorts/groups of children, therefore plan to the needs of the current cohort and not necessarily deliver previous plans without evaluation and amendment.

Partnership with parents

At

we encourage parents and carers to be involved by:

★ asking parents and carers their opinion on this subject via questionnaire

★ inviting parents and carers into our setting to attend an information session on the positive impact of weapon/superhero play and its impact on attainment

★ sending home information about the general benefit of weapon/superhero play and how it is positively impacting on their child

★ encouraging parents and carers to come in and help in the setting.

Continuing Professional Development

◆ The staff in the setting know what the Development Matters and EYFS Profile contain and how to interpret the scale points in relation to role play

◆ All staff are confident in making assessments through the observation of children

◆ Staff plan opportunities for role play collaboratively checking that continuity and progressions are evident and based on children's preferences and interests.

APPENDICES

Could include:

✓ A resources list

✓ An action plan for the development of role play

✓ Examples of weapon/superhero play moderation/impact

✓ References to appropriate relevant information

✓ References to other information/publications about weapon/superhero play.